The Eclectic Sole
Socks for Adventurous Knitters

Janel Laidman

RUSTLING LEAF PRESS

Rustling Leaf Press
P.O. Box 250981
Glendale, CA 91225
www.rustlingleafpress.com

Printed in Canada by Friesens

Laidman, Janel, 1963 -
The Eclectic Sole 2008
ISBN 978-0-9814972-0-4

RUSTLING LEAF PRESS
www.rustlingleafpress.com

For Rustle

and Ruthie

Acknowledgements

Publishing your own book is a labor of love, an act of optimism and a test of discipline. When I began I had no idea of the scope of this adventure, it has been exhilarating. I could not have succeeded without the expert guidance and loving support of friends, family and colleagues.

I owe a large debt of gratitude to Cat Bordhi who mentored me through the process of producing this book. Cat's generous sharing of knowledge, passion and encouragement gave me the bones of my book and allowed me to begin filling in the details. Thank you Cat for giving me the strength and hope to carry it out!

Deb Robson has been an inspiration from afar. Reading her weblog on self publishing has given me insight and ideas and helped me know which questions to ask. Thank you Deb for sharing your knowledge with the world.

The socks and patterns in this book would be nothing without the knitters. The members of the Chameleon Colorworks Sock of the Month club test drove many of the patterns and provided the impetus to keep me on track with my design schedule.

Special thanks to Cookie A., a friend, confidante and fellow sock designer for all the late nights, crazy road trips and good advice.

Grateful appreciation to the biochemistry vixens, Inna, Yingssu and Shiho for their adventurous modeling of the socks. Thanks and appreciation to all the members of the 3rd Visionary Retreat for their gentle listening and enthusiastic support.

Of course, I would be nowhere without the support of my family. Special thanks to my parents Bryce and Wilma Wheeler, and my in-laws Dan Laidman and Sylvia Redleaf, Nancy Parsley and Roberta Laidman. Special thanks to Ruth Laidman for all those Friday night poker parties that made for such good sock knitting!

And the most thanks of all to my sweet, generous, husband Russell who has supported me from the very beginning and enabled me to pursue my dreams.

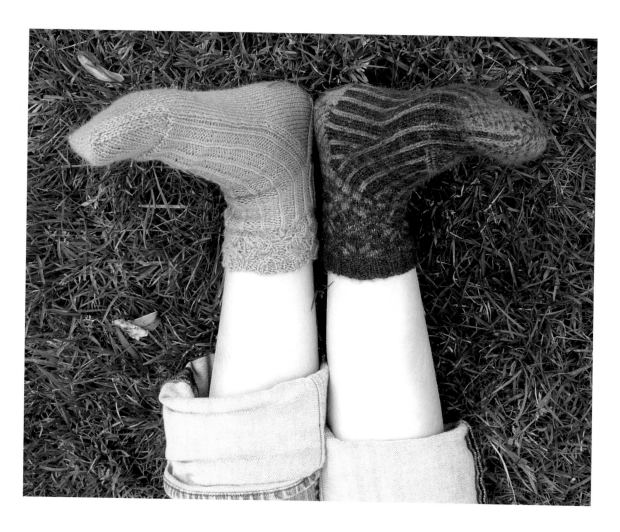

Contents

Introduction...................................... 8

The Socks
    Simplicity.................................. 17
    Niagara....................................21
    Rivendell.................................. 27
    Monterey.................................. 33
    Hydrangea................................. 37
    Nordic Lights............................. 41
    Hypnosis.................................. 47
    Biological Clock......................... 53
    Hope..59
    Migration.................................. 65
    April Fool................................. 69
    Kristallen 75
    Koi... 79
    Josephine.................................. 83

Chart Key and Techniques.............. 86
Resources.. 94

Introduction

Socks, how do I love them? Let me count the ways....

I was trying to figure out why I love knitting socks with such a deep and abiding passion. First of all, socks are a wonderful project for trying out a new technique that you haven't encountered before. They are a compact, portable project that is easy to take with you when visiting, commuting or waiting. Socks are equally satisfying whether they are complicated or simple, and they are a great place to showcase a vibrant yarn that would overwhelm a larger item like a sweater. Socks make a perfect gift, they are both practical and extravagant at the same time; time consuming enough to say "I love you" and yet small enough they can be appropriate for a co-worker. Socks make the perfect alternative to a "boyfriend sweater," and of course they are a wonderful way to say "I love you" to yourself! Socks also make a nice break project when you get tired of knitting on bigger projects; I am never without a sock project on the needles. Best of all, a pair of hand knit socks will always warm the feet as well as the heart. A cold winter morning will cause your recipient to thank you twice, once for each foot!

The Eclectic Sole began as a sock of the month club. Each month I tried to design a sock to showcase a different technique or type of yarn. Some of the socks are simple, others are more challenging. Some socks have a touch of whimsy, others feature a particular technique like colorwork, cables or lace. I approached each design as an adventure, and I hope you will find each one an adventure to knit as well.

8

If You are New to Knitting Socks

A good place to start is with the very first pattern *Simplicity*. This is a basic ribbed sock with a little eyelet pattern for interest. It will introduce you to all of the parts of a top-down sock and get you knitting in the round.

Swatching and Gauge

Socks are such a small project that you can often just start the sock without swatching, just think of your beginning sock as a swatch! Remember to check your gauge in the first few inches to avoid heartache later. The exceptions to this are the sideways knit socks which are knit flat and then grafted together. For these socks you will want to knit a test swatch, to discover your stockinette stitch gauge and your row gauge. Because your knitting tension may change from your knit stitch to your purl stitch, it is a good idea to swatch in the round if you'll be knitting in the round and swatch flat if you'll be knitting flat.

In the socks that are knit in the round, your stitch gauge will be the more important gauge to watch because that will determine the tightness of your sock. For more or less length you will just add or subtract rows. However, the flat knit sideways socks require attention to the row gauge as well as the stitch gauge since you will need to knit a certain number of rows around the foot. You will also calculate how many stitches to knit for the foot and cuff based on your stitch gauge.

The needle size recommended for a particular yarn is always only a recommendation. If you are not getting the correct gauge with the needles you are using you should go up or down in needle size to obtain the correct gauge.

9

Yarn and Fibers

Each pattern carries an information box containing yarn specs for the model depicted. Information on the yarn used in each pattern gives you the brand and color, the fiber content and the weight and WPI of the yarn used. In addition there are color recommendations of "solid", "semi-solid" or "painted". This information should help you substitute suitable yarns to complete the pattern.

All of the socks in this book were knit with wool or wool blend yarn. Most of them are made with a machine washable wool, which is indicated by the word "superwash" on the yarn label. A few socks, however, were knit with regular (not superwash) wool. These socks will need to be washed by hand. This is a decision you can make when you decide which yarns to use in your socks. Although wool sock yarns are the most abundant, there are other wonderful fiber choices including cotton, bamboo, synthetics and blends.

10

WPI = Wraps per Inch

WPI is a method of gauging the *grist* or thickness of a yarn, and is a good method to use when substituting yarn. Because our current yarn "weight" designations come from industry practices and historical terms, they can have obscure meanings which are not always interpreted the same way. A WPI measurement can be a more accurate way to get a grasp on the thickness of the yarn called for without complicating it by thinking about the weight of the fiber or the density at which it was spun. To measure the WPI of a given yarn, wrap the yarn around a ruler or other gauge marked out in inches. The wraps should just touch each other without crowding or gaps. The number of times you can wrap around the ruler in one inch is the WPI number. The higher the number, the thinner the yarn and conversely a small number indicates a thick yarn. Most sock yarns are designated as "fingering" or "sport" weight by yarn manufacturers. To this information you can now add the WPI.

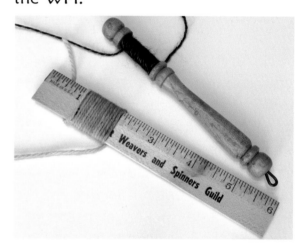

Color, Color, Color

Each pattern has a recommendation for color choices when substituting a yarn. A *solid* color is one that has been commercially dyed and the color is without variation. A *semi-solid* color is usually hand dyed, although you may find some commercial examples as well. This is a color in which the *hue* (color) stays the same but there are changes

semi-solid that is almost a true solid

semi-solid with more value variation

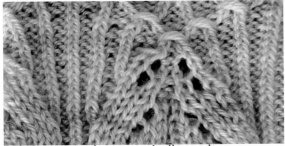
subtle painted yarn - similar values

painted yarn

painted yarn with heathering & longer color repeats

in *value* (lightness and darkness) of the hue. Some semi-solids have subtle variation and others are bold. A *painted* yarn is one that has several different colors. I make a distinction between a subtle painted yarn and a bold painted yarn. A subtle painted yarn will have colors that are either all of the same value or else are *analogous*. Analogous colors are those which are next to each other on the color wheel or which you can think of as in the same color family. For example green, blue and purple are next to each other on the color wheel as are yellow, orange and red. These are examples of analogous color families. With colors of similar value or that are in the same family, the eye blurs the distinction between the colors and therefore the color combination appears more subtle.

The color recommendations for each pattern are made on the principle that complicated stitch patterns show up best in a solid or semi-solid, while simpler sock patterns benefit from the added pizzazz of more color. Keep in mind, however, that the color recommendations are only suggestions. These are your socks, of course, so if you're anxious to try out that new colorway, or you prefer the quieter tones of a solid, then, by all means you should go for the gusto!

11

Double Points or Circulars?

All of the patterns in this book can be knit on either double pointed needles (dpns) or circular needles with the exception of the sideways socks which can be knit on either circulars or straight needles. Each pattern has designated *instep* stitches and *heel* stitches. The instep stitches are the stitches which will make up the front of the sock, the front of the cuff, the top of the foot down to the top of the toes. The heel stitches are the ones that will make up the back of the cuff, encompass the heel or the opening for the heel, and continue on the bottom of the foot down to the underside of the toes.

If you are using dpns, it will be easiest to follow the patterns if you use 4 needles and divide the instep stitches across two needles and the heel stitches across the other two. You will need a fifth needle to work the stitches. If you are using the magic loop method of knitting, you will want to put your instep stitches on one side of the loop and your heel stitches on the other side. If you are knitting with two circular needles, your instep stitches will go on one needle and your heel stitches on the other.

Colorwork

Three of the patterns in this book are stranded colorwork knit in the round. It is important to keep your tension tight enough to have neat stitches, yet loose enough to have some stretch in the resulting knit. I find the easiest way to keep this balance is to knit with one color in my right hand and the other in my left hand. Experiment until you find the right balance in your own colorwork knitting. All of the colorwork socks have relatively short cuffs because colorwork is not as stretchy as stockinette or ribbing and can't encompass the changes in leg diameter as easily without built in shaping.

Sock Anatomy

Socks are basically composed of a tube that is open on one end and closed on the other. In fact, that's exactly what "tube socks" are. In order to make the tubes fit a little better, we design in an outcropping to go over the heel. The sock can be constructed as a tube with an opening left for putting the heel in afterward, or the heel can be knit in as you go along. If a sock is designed in the round from the top down or the toe up, you determine where the heel goes in by measuring it on your foot as you go, or by carefully measuring the foot and calculating based on your row gauge. If a sock is designed sideways, the relative length of the different parts of the tube need to be calculated before you reach the side with the heel opening.

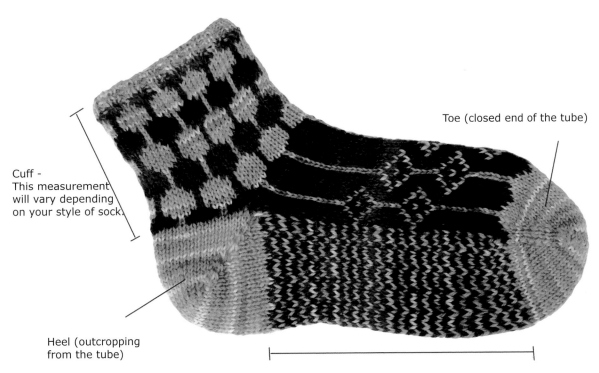

Toe (closed end of the tube)

Cuff -
This measurement will vary depending on your style of sock

Heel (outcropping from the tube)

length of foot from heel to toe. It is important to know this measurement for sideways socks

The Sock Patterns

Simplicity

Fresh and delicate, Simplicity is a perfect place to start! This sock takes a classic K2 P2 rib and adds a little twist with an intermittent eyelet pattern to give it flair. This sock is elastic and comfortable and can easily be made any size. It's a good sock to begin with for those who are new to sock knitting, and its construction is classic top-down knitting in the round with a flap and gusset heel and side decrease toe. This is a great sock for those beautiful painted yarns because the stitch pattern is so simple it can't get lost in the colors! Use a short cuff to make a cute anklet or knit a long cuff and fold it over. Simplicity.

Simplicity Specs

Yarn requirements: approximately 350 yd of fingering weight sock yarn .

Yarn used: Yarn Love Juliet (75% superwash, 25% nylon), color: Limeade & Violet, 1 skein (WPI = 15).

Needles: Size 1 circular or double pointed needles, or size to obtain correct gauge.

Gauge: 8.5 stitches, 12 rounds per inch (2.5 cm) in stockinette.

Notions: Stitch marker, tapestry needle.

Color Suggestions: Solid, Semi-Solid, Painted.

Cast On

Using a long tail cast on, the slip knot cast on, or your favorite flexible cast on, cast on 60 stitches and join in a round taking care not to twist your work.

Cuff

P 1, *K2 P2* repeat the instructions between the ** 14 more times. end with K2 P1.

Continue in K 2 P2 rib for 3 more rounds.

Rounds 5-21:

Follow chart 1 starting at lower right and moving to the left and up. Repeat the chart 15 times around the circumference of the sock. When you reach the end of chart 1, repeat the 8 rows of the chart 3 more times. You should now have completed 36 rounds.

Chart 1

				8
—	—			7
—	—			6
—	—			5
—	—	⋏	O	4
—	—			3
—	—	O	⋋	2
—	—			1

4 3 2 1

Heel

Divide the stitches in half. One half of the stitches is now called "instep," the other half is now called "heel". Instep and Heel stitches are divided according to the following (you may need to move a stitch from one needle to another):

Instep stitches should contain P1, (6)K2P2, ending with K2 P1. (i.e. a K2 P2 rib with one purl stitch on either side, 32 stitches total). Heel stitches should contain 28 stitches in K2 P2 rib with one purl stitch on each side.

Heel Flap:

Continuing in K2 P2 rib, knit only the heel stitches back and forth until heel flap is the correct depth for your heel, this is usually about 2 inches.

Turn Heel:

Row 1: Sl 1, knit until 8 stitches remain on left hand needle, ssk, k1, turn.

Row 2: Sl 1, purl until 8 stitches remain on left hand needle, p2tog, p1, turn.

Row 3: Sl 1, knit until 6 stitches remain on left hand needle (1 st before the gap made by turning), ssk, k1, turn.

Row 4: Sl 1, purl until 6 stitches remain on left hand needle (1 st before the gap made by turning), p2tog, p1, turn.

Row 5: Sl 1, knit until 4 stitches remain on left hand needle (1 st before the gap made by turning), ssk, k1, turn.

Row 6: Sl 1, purl until 4 stitches remain on left hand needle (1 st before the gap made by turning), p2tog, p1, turn.

Row 7: Sl 1, knit until 2 stitches remain on left hand needle (1 st before the gap made by turning), ssk, turn.

Row 8: Sl 1, purl until 2 stitches remain on left hand needle (1 st before the gap made by turning), p2tog, turn,

you are now on RS. You should have 20 heel stitches.

Knit across all 20 heel stitches.

Gusset:

Round 1: With heel needle pick up 15 sts (or appropriate number for your adjusted heel flap depth) on left side of the heel flap you just made.

Work across instep stitches following K2 P2 rib pattern as already established. With a spare needle pick up 15 (or same

18

number you picked up on the left side) stitches on right side of heel flap and transfer to heel needle. Heel stitches now number 52 stitches (or adjusted number based on your heel flap depth and number of picked up stitches). Knit to end of heel stitches.

Round 2:

Instep stitches: continue knitting in K2 P2 rib pattern as already established.
Heel stitches: K1, SSK, K to last 3 sts of needle; k2 tog, K 1.

Round 3:

Instep stitches: continue knitting in K2 P2 rib pattern as already established
Heel stitches: K

Repeat rounds 2 and 3 until you have 30 heel stitches.   You should now have 30 stitches on heel and 30 stitches on instep balanced symmetrically.

Foot:

Instep stitches: Continue in K2 P2 rib pattern as already established.
Heel stitches: K

repeat these two rows until foot is the correct length to begin toe shaping (usually this is at base of big toe).

Toe:

Round 1:

K both instep and heel stitches

Round 2:

Instep stitches: K1, SSK, K to last 3 stitches, K2tog, K1.
Heel stitches: same as instep stitches.

Repeat rounds 1 and 2 until you have 14 stitches per needle. Graft toe closed.

Niagara

The name says it all, romance, beauty, inspiration. For me, the word Niagara evokes a bygone era when the honeymoon of choice was a trip to view this wonder of nature, and ladies wore hats and lacy underthings. In the spirit of those halcyon days, these socks incorporate a frothy, yet simple, lace pattern that gives the feeling of water flowing over the edge and down the sock ending in a delicate point on the foot. Wear them under your sensible trousers as a secret treat or out from under your skirts for the whole world to admire. Knit a little bit of the romance of Niagara for your feet.

Niagara Specs

Yarn requirements: approximately 350 yd of fingering weight sock yarn.

Yarn used: Chameleon Colorworks Footsie (75% superwash, 25% nylon), color: Water, 1 skein (WPI = 16.5)

Needles: Size 1 circular or double pointed needles, or size to obtain correct gauge.

Gauge: 8 stitches and 11 rounds per inch (2.5 cm) in stockinette.

Notions: Stitch marker, tapestry needle.

Color Suggestions: Solid, Semi-solid or subtle painted.

Cast On

Using a long tail cast on, the slip knot cast on, or your favorite flexible cast on, cast on 60 stitches and join in a round taking care not to twist your work.

Cuff

Divide stitches in half and distribute in two sets of stitches, instep sts (30 sts), and heel sts (30 sts).

Rounds 1-64:

Follow chart 1 starting at lower right and moving to the left and up. Repeat the chart 6 times around the circumference of the sock. You will have 3 repeats of the chart per instep and 3 repeats per heel. When you reach the end of chart 1 (row 16), repeat the chart 3 more times.

Heel

Heel flap:

Using just heel stitches, work back and forth (i.e. not in the round) in seed stitch until heel is the correct depth for your foot ending on RS row.

> Seed stitch (even number of stitches):
> Row 1: *K1, P1, repeat from * across.
> Row 2: *P1, K1, repeat from * across(you will be knitting the purled stitches and purling the knit stitches from each previous row)

Turn Heel:

Row 1: Sl 1, knit until 8 stitches remain on left hand needle, ssk, k1, turn.

Row 2: Sl 1, purl until 8 stitches remain on left hand needle, p2tog, p1, turn.

Row 3: Sl 1, knit until 6 stitches remain on left hand needle (1 st before the gap made by turning), ssk, k1, turn.

Row 4: Sl 1, purl until 6 stitches remain on left hand needle (1 st before the gap made by turning), p2tog, p1, turn.

Row 5: Sl 1, knit until 4 stitches remain on left hand needle (1 st before the gap made by turning), ssk, k1, turn.

Row 6: Sl 1, purl until 4 stitches remain on left hand needle (1 st before the gap made by turning), p2tog, p1, turn.

Row 7: Sl 1, knit until 2 stitches remain on left hand needle (1 st before the gap made by turning), ssk, turn.

Row 8: Sl 1, purl until 2 stitches remain on left hand needle (1 st before the gap made by turning), p2tog, turn,

you are now on RS. You should have 22 heel stitches.

Knit across all 22 heel stitches.

Gusset:

<u>Round 1:</u> With needle heel needle pick up 15 sts (or appropriate number for your adjusted heel flap depth) on left side of heel flap. Knit across instep

Chart 1

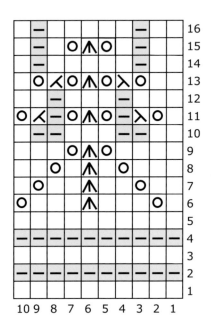

stitches following chart 2 as already established.

With a spare needle pick up 15 (or same number you picked up on the left side) stitches on right side of heel flap and transfer to heel needle. Heel stitches now number 52 stitches (or adjusted number based on your heel flap depth and number of picked up stitches). Knit to end of heel stitches.

Chart 2

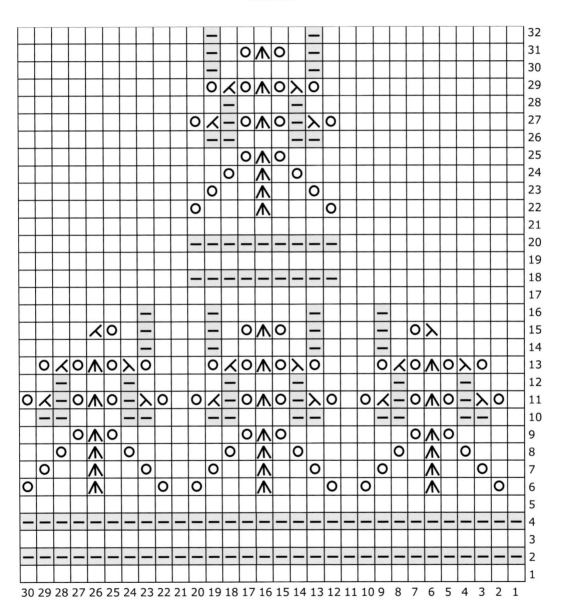

Round 2:

Instep stitches: follow chart 2.
Heel stitches: K1, SSK, K to last 3 sts of needle; k2 tog, K 1.

Round 3:

Instep stitches: follow chart 2.
Heel stitches: K

Round 4-18 :

Repeat rounds 2 and 3 until you have 30 heel stitches remaining.   You should now have 30 stitches on heel and 30 stitches on instep.

24 Foot:

Instep stitches: continue to follow chart 2 until you have completed the chart, thereafter knit stockinette on the instep stitches.
Heel stitches: K

Continue to knit until foot is the correct length to begin toe shaping (usually this is at base of big toe).

Toe:

Round 1:

K both instep and heel stitches

Round 2:

Instep stitches: K1, SSK, K to last 3 stitches, K2tog, K1.
Heel stitches: same as instep stitches.

Repeat rounds 1 and 2 until you have 14 stitches per needle. Graft toe closed.

25

Rivendell

As I was knitting this sock, it began to remind me of a particular Elvish king-dom. It has the same graceful yet strong feel as the art nouveau marbled halls of those lovely folk. This pattern features accentuated ribs and a leafy motif and is as fun to knit as it is to wear. The twisted stitch rib gives the sock extra stretch and compression with a sharply defined rib, the clustered stitches give it a graceful yet strong scallop effect at the top of the cuff. It's the perfect sock for elvish knitters everywhere...

Rivendell Specs

Yarn requirements: approximately 350 yd of fingering weight sock yarn.

Yarn used: Chameleon Colorworks Twinkle Toes (70% superwash merino, 30% tencel), color: Glacial Moraine, 1 skein. (WPI = 19.5)

Needles: Size 1 circular or double pointed needles, or size to obtain correct gauge.

Gauge: 7.5 stitches, 10.5 rounds per inch (2.5 cm) in stockinette.

Notions: Stitch marker, tapestry needle

Color Suggestions: Solid, Semi-Solid, Subtle painted

Cast On

Using a long tail cast on, the slip knot cast on or your favorite flexible cast on, cast on 63 stitches and join in a round.

Cuff

Divide stitches in half and distribute in two sets of stitches, instep sts (32 sts), and heel sts (31 sts). You will adjust these stitches when you get to the heel.

Rounds 1-35: follow chart 1 starting at bottom right and moving left and up. You will have 3 repeats of the chart around the sock's circumference. When row 35 of chart 1 is completed, continue by starting at row 36 of chart 2, starting at the bottom right and working left and up. When row 60 of chart 2 is complete begin heel.

Heel

Set up instep and heel stitches:
Instep stitches = stitches 6 through 21 on first repeat of chart, and stitches 1-16 on second repeat of chart (32 stitches total)
Heel stitches = stitches 17-21 of second

Chart 1

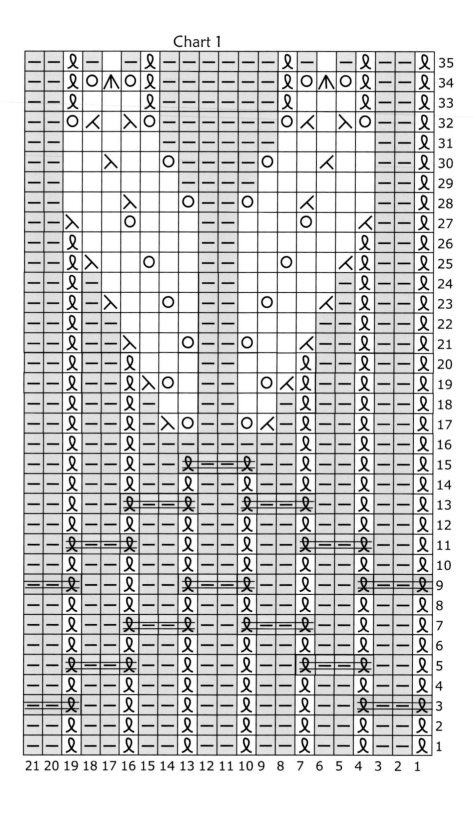

repeat of chart, stitches 1-21 of third repeat of chart and stitches 1-5 of first repeat of chart (31 stitches total)

Heel flap:

Continue K1(b) P2 rib after end of chart 2 on heel stitches only, until heel is the correct depth for your foot (approx 2 inches) ending on RS row.

Turn Heel:

Row 1: Sl 1, knit until 8 stitches remain on left hand needle, ssk, k1, turn.

Row 2: Sl 1, purl until 8 stitches remain on left hand needle, p2tog, p1, turn.

Row 3: Sl 1, knit until 6 stitches remain on left hand needle (1 st before the gap made by turning), ssk, k1, turn.

Row 4: Sl 1, purl until 6 stitches remain on left hand needle (1 st before the gap made by turning), p2tog, p1, turn.

Row 5: Sl 1, knit until 4 stitches remain on left hand needle (1 st before the gap made by turning), ssk, k1, turn.

Row 6: Sl 1, purl until 4 stitches remain on left hand needle (1 st before the gap made by turning), p2tog, p1, turn.

Row 7: Sl 1, knit until 2 stitches remain on left hand needle (1 st before the gap made by turning), ssk, turn.

Row 8: Sl 1, purl until 2 stitches remain on left hand needle (1 st before the gap made by turning), p2tog, turn, you are now on RS. You should have 23 heel stitches.

Knit across all 23 heel stitches.

Gusset:

Round 1:

With heel needle pick up 15 sts (or proper number for your adjusted heel flap depth) on left side of heel flap. Knit instep stitches, following K1(b) P2 rib pattern as already established.

Chart 2

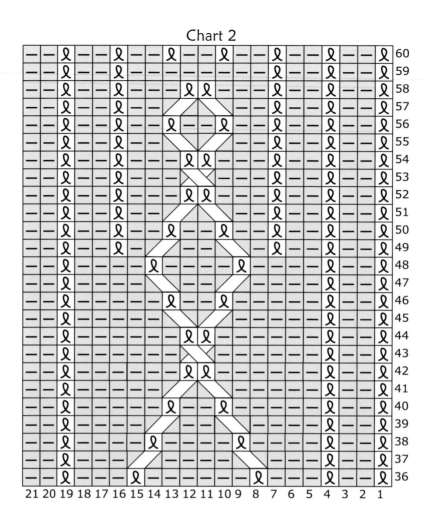

21 20 19 18 17 16 15 14 13 12 11 10 9 8 7 6 5 4 3 2 1

30

With a spare needle pick up 15 (or same number you picked up on the left side) stitches on right side of heel flap and transfer to heel needle.   Heel stitches now number 53 stitches (or adjusted number based on your heel flap depth and number of picked up stitches). Knit to end of heel stitches.

Round 2:

Instep stitches: continue in K1 tbl, P2 ribbing.
Heel stitches: K1, SSK, K to last 3 sts of needle; k2 tog, K 1.

Round 3:

Instep stitches: continue in K1 tbl, P2 ribbing.
Heel stitches: K

Repeat rounds 2 and 3 until you have 31 heel stitches.   You should now have 31 heel stitches and 32 instep stitches.

Foot

Continue in K1 tbl, P2 ribbing on instep stitches, K stockinette on heel stitches, until foot is the correct length to begin toe decreases (usually this is at base of big toe).

Toe:

Round 1:

K both instep and heel stitches

Round 2:

Instep stitches: K1, SSK, K to last 3 stitches, K2tog, K1.
Heel stitches: same as instep stitches.

Repeat rounds 1 and 2 until you have 13 heel stitches and 14 instep stitches. Graft toe closed, starting with first instep stitch and ending with last instep stitch.

A note about stitch clusters....

Chart 1 has two symbols for stitch clusters, a yellow symbol for a 4 stitch cluster and blue symbol for a 7 stitch cluster. Although the blue symbols occur at the edges of the chart, they are to be combined with the blue symbol of the next chart repeat to make a 7 stitch cluster. When the 7 stitch cluster occurs at the beginning of the round, slip the last 3 stitches of the previous round onto the left needle and make the cluster at the beginning of the round. At the end of the round, slip the 3 stitches back.

31

Monterey

Monterey is a beautiful seaside city on the California coast. The area features wide ocean vistas, wild twisted pines and gorgeous golden rocks, all of them decorated with the lace of sea foam. This sock was inspired by the lovely colors of the Trekking yarn I used, which were reminiscent of Monterey. I wanted the colors to look more like a watery landscape, than a striped sock, so I chose to knit the sock sideways and I included whimsical openings that reminded me of bubbles and sea foam. This sock would look equally cute over a pair of tights in the winter, or with sandals and summery frock by the seaside!

Monterey Specs

Yarn requirements: approximately 350 yd of fingering weight sock yarn.

Yarn used: Zitron Trekking XXL (100% superwash wool), color 155, 1 skein (WPI = 18.5)

Needles: Size 1 circular or straight needles, or size to obtain correct gauge.

Gauge: 7 stitches, 11.5 rows per inch (2.5 cm) in stockinette.

Notions: Stitch marker, tapestry needle.

Color Suggestions: hand painted yarns.

Calculate Foot Length:

Using a hand knit sock that fits you well, measure the distance from the beginning of the heel to the beginning of the toe decreases on the bottom of the foot (see diagram in the introduction, page 13). Because you are knitting the sock sideways this is not a readily adjustable area and it needs to be calculated ahead of time.

When you have determined how many inches you need, multiply by 7 (your stitch gauge per inch) to determine how many stitches will make up the bottom of your foot.

With waste yarn, provisionally cast on your number of foot stitches plus 45 [for size 7 ladies I used 80 stitches total, 35 for foot and 45 for leg] stitches. K 3 rows stockinette.

Important Tip:
When looking at the knitting from the right side, the left hand edge of your knitting will end up as the top of your

sock. Knit these stitches loosely to give yourself maximum ease at the top of the sock.

The hole pattern is divided in two sections:

Pattern Section A (right side):

K 3, cast off 5, *K 5, cast off 5* repeat from * until end of row. Because your number of stitches may vary from the model based on the calculations for your own foot, you may not have space to cast off 5 stitches, with at least two stitches left over, at the end of your row. If you don't have space to cast off 5 before the end of the row, just knit stockinette to end of row.

Back side return:
Purl until you reach the cast off portion from the previous row.

*Cast on 5 stitches using the slip stitch cast on or another cast on that doesn't require a long tail, purl 5. Repeat from * until the end of the row ending with purl 3 instead of purl 5.

K 4 rows stockinette

Pattern Section B (right side):

K 8, cast off 5, *K 5, cast off 5* repeat from * until end of row. If you

don't have space to cast off 5 before the end of the row, just k stockinette to end of row.

Back side return:
Purl until you reach the cast off portion from the previous row.

*Cast on 5 stitches using the slip stitch cast on or another cast on that doesn't require a long tail, purl 5. Repeat from * until the end of the row ending with purl

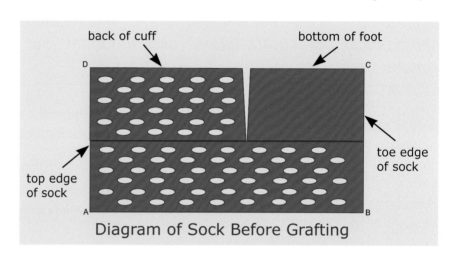

back of cuff   bottom of foot

D   C

top edge of sock

toe edge of sock

A   B

Diagram of Sock Before Grafting

8 instead of purl 5

K 4 rows stockinette

Repeat Pattern Section A followed by Pattern Section B 2 more times (3 times total, 6 pattern sections total)

Divide for foot and cuff:

Knit bottom of foot: With RS facing you, knit the number of stitches you calculated for your foot length (see above) [for size 7 ladies we used 35 stitches]. Do not knit the rest of the stitches on the needle. Turn and purl back Continue on in stockinette stitch for another 36 rows (38 rows total).

Move foot stitches to a piece of waste yarn to hold in place while you knit cuff.

Finish back of cuff:

Continue working 45 (or your adjusted number) cuff stitches in established pattern (Pattern Section A followed by Pattern section B for 3 more repeats of each pattern section.

Graft sock into a tube:

Add all stitches onto the same needle and k 1 row stockinette.
Lay sock on table with right side face down. Fold foot section and cuff section over so that corner A and D touch and corners B and C touch, and instep stitches are facing the table and bottom of foot and back of cuff are face up. Your provisional cast on is at the bottom face down. Remove provisional cast on yarn and place live stitches on a circular needle or piece of yarn.

Graft entire length of sock closed.

Toe:

At toe end of sock, pick up 56 st evenly spaced. 28 instep stitches and 28 heel stitches.

Round 1: K
Round 2:
Instep stitches: K1, SSK, K to last 3 stitches, K2tog, K1. *Heel stitches*: repeat instep stitches.

Repeat rounds 1 and 2 until you have 14 instep and 14 heel stitches. Graft toe closed.

Heel:

At heel opening in sock, pick up 56 st evenly spaced. 28 at top of heel and 28 at bottom of heel. Make sure to pick up corner stitches.

Round 1: K
Round 2:

Top stitches: K2, SSK, K to last 4 stitches, K2tog, K2.

Bottom stitches: Repeat needle 1 stitches

Repeat rounds 1 and 2 until you have 14 stitches per needle. Graft heel closed.

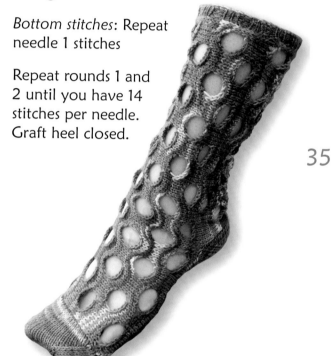

Cuff Ribbing:

At top of cuff Pick up 64 st spaced evenly, 32 instep stitches and 32 heel stitches. K2 P2 rib for 6 rounds. Bind off using sewn bind off.

Hydrangea

Hydrangeas are some of my favorite flowers. I love the way the color of the blossoms will change depending on the mineral content of the soil. These sweet little anklets combine a soft floral border with simple ribbed stems proceeding down the foot. The sock could easily be extended to make a longer cuff if you desire. The soft colors and gradual changes of the Jojoland wool add to the hydrangea-like qualities of this sock. The pattern is simple, and once the chart is complete this sock becomes a knit anywhere pattern.

Hydrangea Specs

Yarn requirements: approximately 300 yd of fingering weight sock yarn.

Yarn used: Jojoland Melody (100% wool), color: 7-y25, 2 balls (WPI = 17)

Needles: Size 1 circular or double pointed needles, or size to obtain correct gauge.

Gauge: 7.5 stitches, 11 rounds per inch (2.5 cm) in stockinette.

Notions: Stitch marker, tapestry needle.

Color Suggestions: Solid or semi-solid.

Cast On

Using a long tail cast on, the slip knot cast on, or your favorite flexible cast on, cast on 64 stitches and join in a round, taking care not to twist your work.

Cuff

Divide stitches in half and distribute in two sets of stitches, instep sts (32 sts), and heel sts (32 sts).

K2 P2 rib for 6 rounds.

Rounds 1-16: follow chart 1 starting at bottom right and moving left and up. You will have 4 repeats of the chart around the sock's circumference. When chart is completed, continue in K1 TBL, P3 rib for 18 rows or as many as necessary to get the cuff length desired.

Heel

Heel Flap:

Heel is knit back and forth on heel stitches only (i.e. not in the round)

Row 1: *sl 1, k1 repeat from * to end of row ending with K1

Row 2: sl 1 p to end of row

Row 3: sl 2, *k1, sl 1 repeat from * until 2 stitches before end of row. End with K2

Row 4: repeat row 2

Repeat rows 1-4 until heel flap is desired length for your foot.

Turn Heel:

Row 1: Sl 1, knit until 8 stitches remain on left hand needle, ssk, k1, turn.

Row 2: Sl 1, purl until 8 stitches remain on left hand needle, p2tog, p1, turn.

Row 3: Sl 1, knit until 6 stitches remain on left hand needle (1 st before the gap made by turning), ssk, k1, turn.

Row 4: Sl 1, purl until 6 stitches remain on left hand needle (1 st before the gap made by turning), p2tog, p1, turn.

Row 5: Sl 1, knit until 4 stitches remain on left hand needle (1 st before the gap made by turning), ssk, k1, turn.

Row 6: Sl 1, purl until 4 stitches remain on left hand needle (1 st before the gap made by turning), p2tog, p1, turn.

Row 7: Sl 1, knit until 2 stitches remain on left hand needle (1 st before the gap made by turning), ssk, turn.

Row 8: Sl 1, purl until 2 stitches remain on left hand needle (1 st before the gap made by turning), p2tog, turn,

you are now on RS. You should have 24 heel stitches.

Knit across all 24 heel stitches.

Gusset:

Round 1:

With heel needle pick up 15 sts (or proper number for your adjusted heel flap depth) on left side of heel flap.

Work instep stitches following K1 TBL, P3 rib pattern as already established,

With a spare needle pick up 15 (or same number you picked up on the left side) stitches on right side of heel flap and transfer to heel needle. Heel stitches now number 54 stitches (or adjusted

38

number based on your heel flap depth and number of picked up stitches). Knit to end of heel stitches.

Round 2:

Instep stitches: Work following K1 TBL, P3 rib pattern as already established, *Heel stitches:* K1, SSK, K to last 3 sts of needle; k2 tog, K 1.

Round 3:

Instep stitches: Work following K1 TBL, P3 rib pattern as already established, *Heel stitches:* K stockinette.

Remaining heel rounds:

Repeat rounds 2 and 3 until you have 28 stitches on heel needle(s).   You should now have 28 stitches on heel needle(s) and 32 stitches on instep needle(s).

Foot:

Continue K1 TBL, P3 rib on instep stitches, K stockinette on heel stitches, until foot is the correct length to begin toe decreases (usually this is at base of big toe).

Toe:

Adjust stitches by slipping first and last instep stitches to heel stitches (30 st each).

Round 1:

K both instep and heel stitches

Round 2:

Instep stitches: K1, SSK, K to last 3 stitches, K2tog, K1.
Heel stitches: same as instep stitches.

Repeat rounds 1 and 2 until you have 14 instep and 14 heel stitches. Graft toe closed.

Chart 1

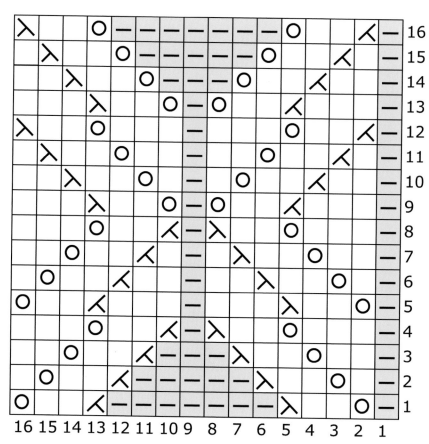

Nordic Lights

I have always wanted to see the Aurora Borealis, but so far I have not yet had that pleasure. The coloring in the yarn used for these socks reminded me of that Northern sky magic. The socks are knit in stranded colorwork, so they are extra cushiony and warm, just as you'd want them to be in frozen climes. The motifs are a combination of traditional Scandinavian snowflake patterns and my own whimsical impulses. These socks are rich with ever changing patterns that will keep you entertained as you cozy up to knit them on a grey winter's day.

Nordic Lights Specs

Yarn requirements: approximately 200 yd each of 2 colors of fingering weight sock yarn.

Yarn used: Zitron Trekking XXL (100% superwash wool) color 76, Zitron Trekking XXL (100% superwash wool) color 146 (WPI = 18.5)

Needles: Size 1 circular or double pointed needles, or size to obtain correct gauge.

Gauge: 8.5 stitches, 10 rounds per inch (2.5 cm) in 2 color stranded knitting.

Notions: Stitch marker, tapestry needle.

Color Suggestions: One solid, one hand painted or two solids or semi-solids.

Cast On

Using a long tail cast on, the slip knot cast on, or your favorite flexible cast on, cast on 64 stitches and join in a round, being careful not to twist work.

Cuff:

Divide stitches in half and distribute in two sets of stitches, instep sts (32 sts), and heel sts (32 sts).

Work K2 P2 ribbing for 9 rounds.

Increase to 72 stitches spaced evenly (i.e., increase by 4 heel and 4 instep sts).

Rounds 1-25: Join color 2. Working in stranded color knitting, follow chart 1 starting at bottom right and moving left and up. You will have 3 repeats of the chart around the sock's circumference.

Rounds 26-28: Follow chart 2 starting at bottom right and moving left and up. You will have 24 repeats of the chart around the sock's circumference.

Round 29: In color 1, K.

chart 1

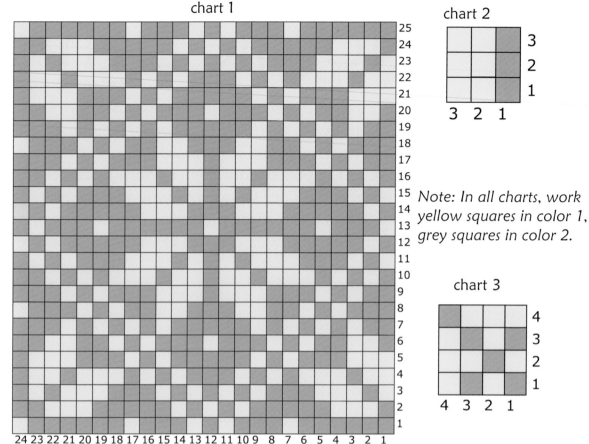

chart 2

3
2
1

3 2 1

Note: In all charts, work yellow squares in color 1, grey squares in color 2.

chart 3

4
3
2
1

4 3 2 1

Heel:

Heel flap:

Follow chart 3 starting at the bottom right and move to the left and up. Work back and forth (i.e. not in the round) until heel flap is the correct depth for your heel (approx. 5 vertical repeats of chart).

Turn Heel:

Work heel turn in color 2.

Row 1: Sl 1, knit until 8 stitches remain on left hand needle, ssk, k1, turn.

Row 2: Sl 1, purl until 8 stitches remain on left hand needle, p2tog, p1, turn.

Row 3: Sl 1, knit until 6 stitches remain on left hand needle (1 st before the gap made by turning), ssk, k1, turn.

Row 4: Sl 1, purl until 6 stitches remain on left hand needle (1 st before the gap made by turning), p2tog, p1, turn.

Row 5: Sl 1, knit until 4 stitches remain on left hand needle (1 st before the gap made by turning), ssk, k1, turn.

Row 6: Sl 1, purl until 4 stitches remain on left hand needle (1 st before the gap made by turning), p2tog, p1, turn.

Row 7: Sl 1, knit until 2 stitches remain on left hand needle (1 st before the gap made by turning), ssk, turn.

Row 8: Sl 1, purl until 2 stitches remain on left hand needle (1 st before the gap made by turning), p2tog, turn,

you are now on RS. You should have 28 heel stitches.

Knit across all 28 heel stitches.
Gusset:

Round 1: With a spare needle, pick up 16 sts on left side of heel flap in the following stripe color pattern:

Stripe pattern: *K3 in color 1, K1 in color 2*.

If you wish to pick up a corner st, it must be one of the 16 sts picked up or it must be decreased immediately; to maintain and properly center the stripe pattern, sts must be picked up in a perfect multiple of 4.

Continue to work stripe pattern across instep stitches.

chart 4

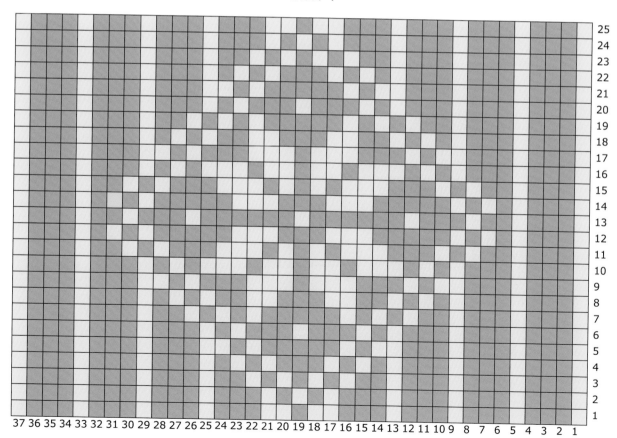

Pick up 16 stitches on right side of heel flap following stripe color pattern:

Continue stripe pattern across heel stitches. You now have 36 instep stitches and 60 heel stitches (96 stitches total). Slip last stitch from heel stitches to instep stitches, you now have 37 instep stitches and 61 heel stitches.

Round 2:

Instep stitches: continue in stripe pattern as already established.
Heel stitches: K1, SSK, K (following established stripe pattern) to last 3 sts of needle; k2 tog, K 1.

Round 3:

Instep stitches: continue in stripe pattern as already established.

Heel stitches: continue in stripe pattern as already established.

Repeat rounds 2 and 3 until you have 31 heel stitches. You should now have 31 heel stitches and 37 instep stitches.

Foot:

Instep stitches: Follow chart 4 beginning at lower right and moving to the left and up.
Heel stitches: Continue following established stripe pattern.

When chart 4 is complete continue in established stripe pattern until foot is the correct length to begin toe decreases (usually this is at base of big toe).

44

chart 5

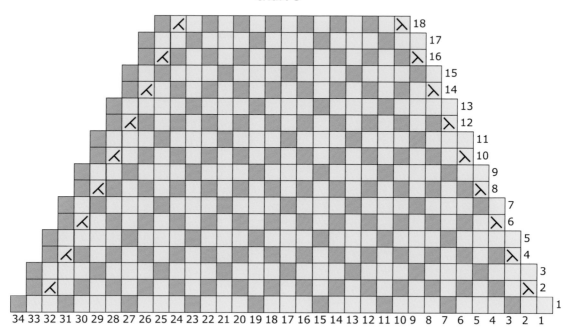

Toe:

Set up round: Slip first 2 stitches from instep stitches to heel stitches. Work across instep stitches in stripe pattern as already established. Slip last instep stitch to heel stitches. You should now have 34 instep stitches and 34 heel stitches. Work across heel stitches in stripe pattern as already established.

Rounds 1-18: Starting on instep stitches, Follow chart 5 starting at the lower right and moving to the left and up, for toe decreases.

When chart 5 is complete, graft toe closed.

Hypnosis

You are getting sleeeeeeeeeeeeeepy... When I was a child I had a definition of hypnosis in my head that was based on campy 60's Batman TV shows and stage acts that left people squawking like a chicken. Invariably the hypnosis was induced by a twirly swirly pattern spinning in front of the patient's eyes. Although I never ended up clucking or squawking, I always loved to stare at the twirly swirlys, and this sock is a reminder of those types of patterns. The undulating rib pattern gives a sense of motion throughout the sock, and, although the chart looks big, the pattern is easy to learn. Best of all, the rib pattern gives the sock the same stretchy, snug fit as a plain vanilla ribbed sock, but the twirly swirlys makes it feel fancy.

Hypnosis Specs

Yarn requirements: approximately 350 yd of fingering weight sock yarn.

Yarn used: Chameleon Colorworks footsie (75% superwash wool, 25% nylon), color: Peacock (WPI = 16.5)

Needles: Size 1 circular or double pointed needles, or size to obtain correct gauge.

Gauge: 8 stitches, 11 rounds per inch (2.5 cm) in stockinette.

Notions: Stitch marker, tapestry needle.

Color Suggestions: Semi-solid or painted.

Cast On

Using a long tail cast on, the slip knot cast on, or your favorite flexible cast on, cast on 60 stitches and join in a round, taking care not to twist your work.

Cuff

Distribute stitches in two sets of stitches, instep sts (31 sts), and heel sts (29 sts).

Rounds 1-44:

Follow chart 1 starting at lower right and moving to the left and up. Repeat the chart 2 times around the circumference of the sock,

Instep stitches encompass stitches 1-30 of the first repeat and stitch 1 of the second repeat. Heel stitches encompass stitches 2-30 of the second repeat.

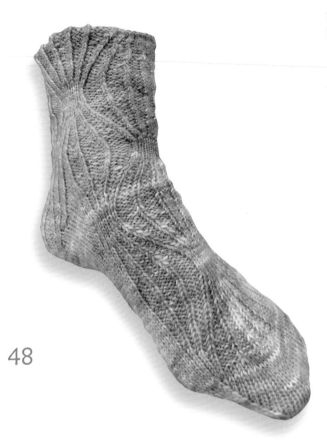

When you have completed chart 1, repeat rows 1 and 2 of the chart before beginning heel.

Heel

Heel flap:

At row 3 of chart 1 continue chart on heel stitches only (knitting back and forth). until heel is the correct depth for your foot ending on RS row.

Turn Heel:

Row 1: Sl 1, knit until 8 stitches remain on left hand needle, ssk, k1, turn.

Row 2: Sl 1, purl until 8 stitches remain on left hand needle, p2tog, p1, turn.

Row 3: Sl 1, knit until 6 stitches remain on left hand needle (1 st before the gap made by turning), ssk, k1, turn.

Row 4: Sl 1, purl until 6 stitches remain on left hand needle (1 st before the gap made by turning), p2tog, p1, turn.

Row 5: Sl 1, knit until 4 stitches remain on left hand needle (1 st before the gap made by turning), ssk, k1, turn.

Row 6: Sl 1, purl until 4 stitches remain on left hand needle (1 st before the gap made by turning), p2tog, p1, turn.

Row 7: Sl 1, knit until 2 stitches remain on left hand needle (1 st before the gap made by turning), ssk, turn.

Row 8: Sl 1, purl until 2 stitches remain on left hand needle (1 st before the gap made by turning), p2tog, turn,

you are now on RS. You should have 21 heel stitches.

Knit across all 21 heel stitches.

Gusset:

Round 1:

With heel needle pick up 15 sts (or appropriate number for your adjusted heel flap depth) on left side of the heel flap you just made.

Work across instep stitches following chart 1 as already established.

With a spare needle pick up 15 (or same number you picked up on the left side) stitches on right side of heel flap and transfer to heel needle.

Heel stitches now number 51 stitches (or adjusted number based on your heel flap depth and number of picked up stitches). Knit to end of heel stitches.

Round 2:

Instep stitches: continue working according to chart 1 pattern as already established.
Heel stitches: K1, SSK, K to last 3 sts of needle; k2 tog, K 1.

Round 3:

Instep stitches: continue working according to chart 1 pattern as already established.
Heel stitches: K

Repeat rounds 2 and 3 until you have 29 heel stitches.   You should now have 29 stitches on heel and 31 stitches on instep. Slip first stitch from instep to heel.

Foot:

Instep stitches: Continue working according to chart 1 pattern as already established.
Heel stitches: K

Continue to work until foot is the correct length to begin toe shaping (usually this is at base of big toe).

Toe:

Round 1:

K both instep and heel stitches

Round 2:

Instep stitches: K1, SSK, K to last 3 stitches, K2tog, K1.
Heel stitches: same as instep stitches.

49

Repeat rounds 1 and 2 until you have 14 instep and 14 heel stitches. Graft toe closed.

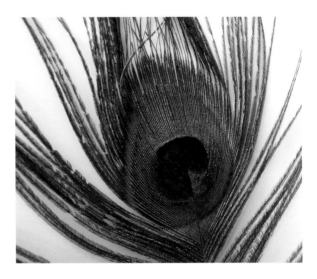

Chart 1

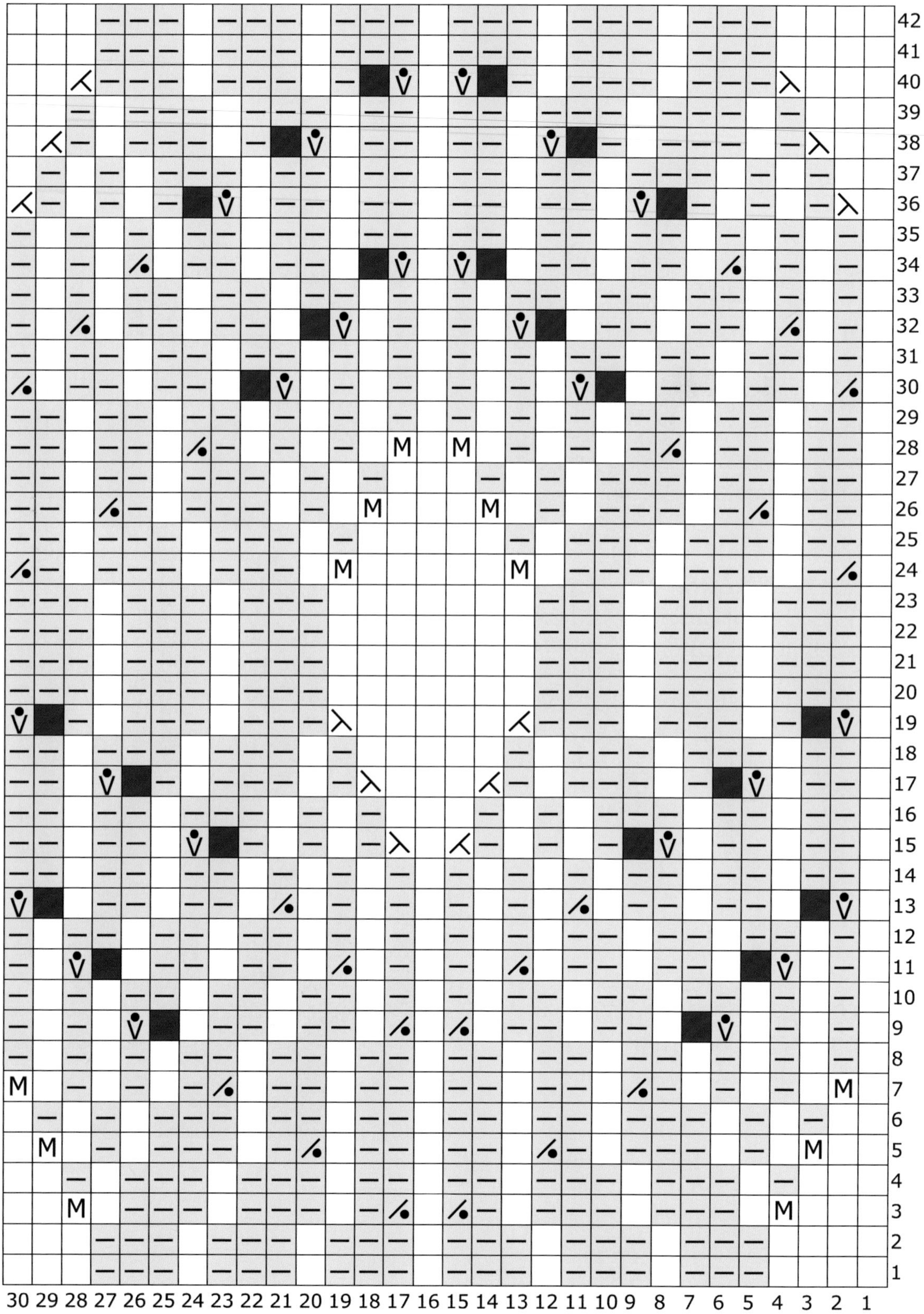

Biological Clock

This sock incorporates a visual pun that makes them extra fun for the true knitterati. Clocks are fancy patterns that run up the side of socks to help introduce shaping to the leg of the sock through judicious use of decreasing and increasing. This clock for this sock has a pattern of a DNA double helix running up the side making it a "biological" clock! The sock is knit from the toe up and incorporates a reverse flap and gusset heel, giving the great fit of that style of heel with the practicality of a toe-up construction. The leg ends in a sweet picot edge that gives the sock a little feminine touch and a nice strong cuff. Time is ticking...

Biological Clock Specs

Yarn requirements: approximately 350 yd of fingering weight sock yarn.

Yarn used: Chameleon Colorworks Bambino (30% Bamboo, 70% superwash Merino), color: Pistachio, 1 skein. (WPI = 15.5)

Needles: Size 1 circular or double pointed needles, or size to obtain correct gauge.

Gauge: 8.5 stitches, 12 rounds per inch (2.5 cm) in stockinette.

Notions: Stitch marker, tapestry needle.

Color Recommendations: Solid or Semi-solid.

Cast On:

Holding two needles together, cast on 15 stitches using a figure 8 cast on. Knit one side of the cast on with one needle and then the other side with a second needle. You now have 15 live stitches on either side of the cast on. One set of 15 is your instep stitches, and the other set is the heel sts (30 sts total).

Toe:

Round 1: Knit instep and heel stitches
Round 2: On instep stitches K1, M1, K to one stitch before last stitch, M1, K1 repeat on heel stitches
Rounds 3-16: repeat rounds 1 and 2 until you have 31 instep and 31 heel stitches.

Foot:

work both instep and heel stitches in stockinette until the sock has reached approx. 2.5 inches from heel. Measure by trying the sock on your foot. At this point you will begin the gusset.

Gusset:

Round 1:

Instep stitches: work stockinette stitch.

Heel stitches: K1, M1, knit across remaining heel stitches until only 1 heel stitch remains, M1, K1.

Round 2:

Instep and heel stitches: work stockinette stitch.

Repeat rounds 1 and 2 until you have 54 heel stitches. Work 12 heel stitches, place marker, work 30 heel stitches place marker, work rest of round. Your heel stitches are now divided into 12 stitches, 30 stitches and 12 stitches.

Turn Heel:

Work first 12 stitches of heel stitches to first marker.

Row 1: Knit 29 stitches. Bring yarn to front as if to purl and slip last stitch from left needle to right needle. Turn your work.

Row 2: Move yarn to front again as if to purl. Slip first stitch from left needle to right needle (the stitch that was

unworked from the previous row). Purl next stitch. The yarn that you brought forward on the previous row and then forward on this row will have completely wrapped around the last stitch. This is called a wrap.

Purl across until one stitch remains unpurled. Bring yarn to back as if to knit and slip last stitch. Turn your work.

Row 3: Bring yarn to back as if to knit. Slip first stitch. You have wrapped that stitch. Knit across to the last stitch before the unworked stitch. Wrap and turn your work.

Row 4: Slip first stitch, purl across to stitch before the unworked stitch. Wrap and turn.

Repeat row 3 and 4 until you have 5 wrapped stitches on either end and 20 live stitches in the middle.

Finish heel turn:

Row 1: Knit all live stitches to the first wrapped stitch. Pick up the wrap and the stitch and knit them together. Pick up the next wrapped stitch and wrap and knit them together. Continue to pick up wrapped stitches and wraps and knit together until you reach the marker. Turn your work.

Row 2: Slip the first stitch. Purl across to the first wrapped stitch. Pick up stitch and wrap and purl together. Continue to pick up stitches and wraps and purl together until you reach the marker. Turn your work

Pick up flap:

Row 1: Slip the first stitch,*K1, sl 1. repeat from * until one stitch before marker. K last stitch before marker and first stitch after marker together (you will have to move marker one stitch to left to avoid trapping the marker. Turn work

Row 2: Slip the first stitch, ,*P1, sl 1. repeat from * until one stitch before marker. P last stitch before marker and first stitch after marker together (you will have to move marker one stitch to left to avoid trapping the marker. Turn work.

Repeat rows 1 and 2 until all side stitches have been picked up. You should now have 30 heel stitches and 30 instep stitches.

Knit one entire round.

Chart 2

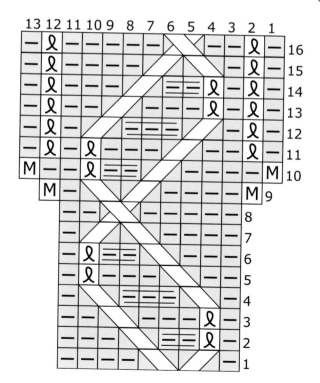

Chart 1

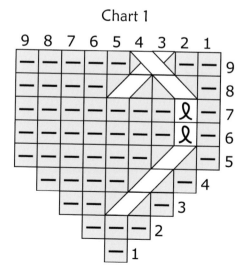

Leg

Rearrange needles so that you now have a left side and right side rather than instep and heel stitches. You have 2 sets of stitches, hereafter referred to as *left side* and *right side*.

Round 1:

Left and right sides: K 15, place marker, K 16

Begin chart 1:

Rounds 1-9

Left and right sides: Centering chart 1 right after the stitch marker, K stockinette until you reach the chart stitches, then follow chart 1, then continue to K stockinette to end of side.

56

Chart 3

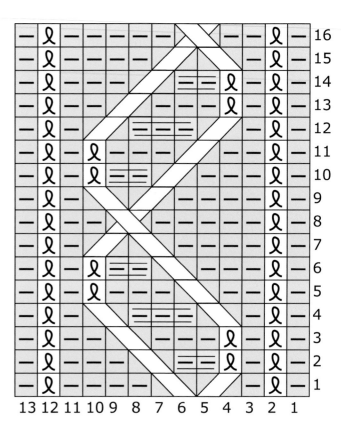

13 12 11 10 9 8 7 6 5 4 3 2 1

Chart 4

17 16 15 14 13 12 11 10 9 8 7 6 5 4 3 2 1

12
11
10
9
8
7
6
5
4
3
2
1

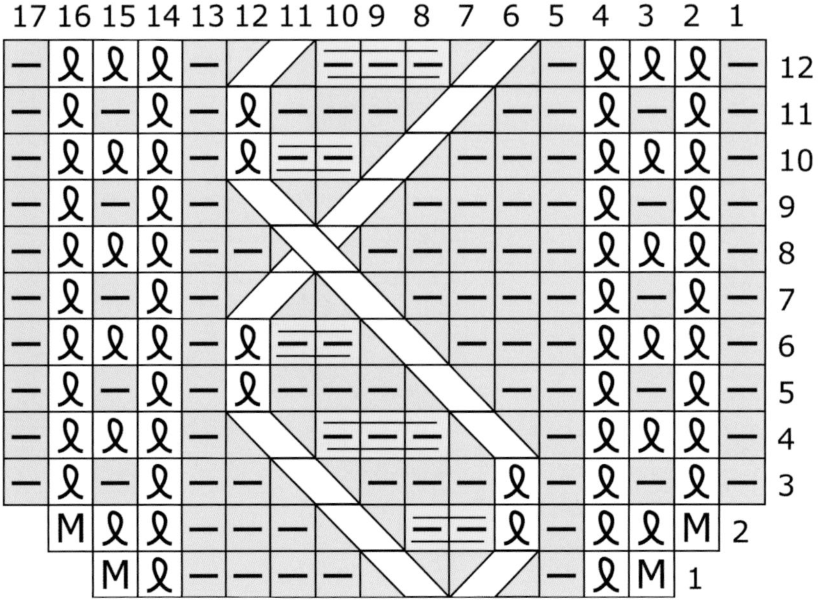

Rounds 10-25

Left and right sides: Continuing in the same manner, center chart 2 above chart 1. K stockinette until you reach the chart stitches, then follow chart 2, then continue to K stockinette to end of side.

Rounds 26-42

Left and right sides: Continuing in the same manner, center chart 3 above chart 2. K stockinette until you reach the chart stitches, then follow chart 3, then continue to K stockinette to end of side.

Rounds 43-55

Left and right sides: Continuing in the same manner, center chart 4 above chart 3. K stockinette until you reach the chart stitches, then follow chart 4, then continue to K stockinette to end of side.

Cuff

Picot edge:

Round 1-5: K stockinette

Round 6: *YO, K2tog repeat from * to end of round

Round 7-10: K1 P1 rib

Bind off

Move live stitches to waste yarn. Fold ribbing to inside with fold at YO row to form picot edge. Stitch live stitches to cuff being careful to avoid waste yarn. Remove waste yarn and darn in end.

57

Hope

I got a call last year telling me that a good friend of mine was diagnosed with breast cancer. I needed a way to show her that I loved her and was thinking of her and that I carried hope in my heart for her prognosis. Nearly all of us have been touched by this disease or by other causes affecting us or the ones we love. This pattern was begun as an expression of love and hope for her and everyone suffering from this disease. Every time I wear my pair of these socks I think of my friend, and each time she wears her pair of them I hope she feels the love I send her. Make these socks in whatever color is appropriate for your message of hope. They are soft and cushy with the right amount of stretch to make them feel gently supportive.

Hope Specs

Yarn requirements: approximately 350 yd of fingering weight sock yarn.

Yarn used: Chameleon Colorworks Bambino (30% Bamboo, 70% superwash merino), color: Rose (WPI = 15.5)

Needles: Size 1 circular or double pointed needles, or size to obtain correct gauge.

Gauge: 8.5 stitches, 12 rounds per inch (2.5 cm) in stockinette.

Notions: Stitch marker, tapestry needle.

Color Suggestions: solids, semi solids, subtle painted.

Cast on:

Using a long tail cast on, the slip knot cast on, or your favorite flexible cast on, cast on 60 stitches and join in a round, taking care not to twist your work. K3, P1 for 8 rounds.

Cuff:

Increase evenly around cuff by 4 stitches to 64 stitches. Divide stitches into 39 instep and 25 heel stitches.

Rounds 1-39:

Instep stitches follow chart 1 starting at bottom right and moving to the left and up. At row 10 of chart 1, instep stitches will increase to 40.

Heel stitches follow chart 2 starting at bottom right and moving to the left and up.

Chart 1

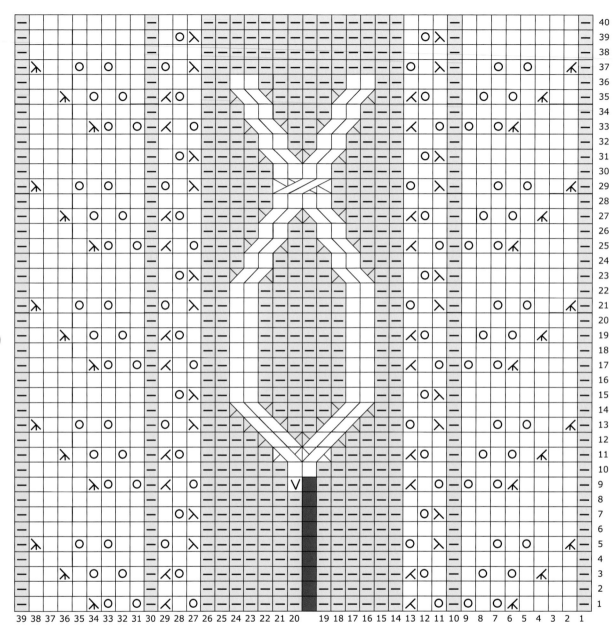

60

Heel:

Heel Flap

On heel stitches only continue following chart 2 for 18 rows or until heel flap is correct depth for your foot.

Turn Heel:

Row 1: Sl 1, knit until 6 stitches remain on left hand needle, ssk, k1, turn.

Row 2: Sl 1, purl until 6 stitches remain on left hand needle, p2tog, p1, turn.

Row 3: Sl 1, knit until 4 stitches remain on left hand needle (1 st before the gap made by turning), ssk, k1, turn.

Row 4: Sl 1, purl until 4 stitches remain on left hand needle (1 st before the gap made by turning), p2tog, p1, turn.

Row 5: Sl 1, knit until 2 stitches remain on left hand needle (1 st before the gap made by turning), ssk, turn.

Row 6: Sl 1, purl until 2 stitches remain on left hand needle (1 st before the gap made by turning), p2tog, turn. You are now on RS. You should have 19 heel stitches.

Knit across all 19 heel stitches.

Gusset:

Round 1:

With heel needle pick up 9 sts on left side of heel flap

Work instep stitches, following line 40 of chart 1. With a spare needle pick up 9 stitches on right side of heel flap and transfer to heel needle. Knit to end of heel stitches.

Chart 2

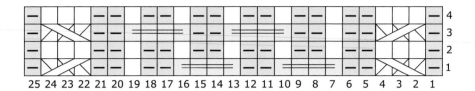

Chart 3

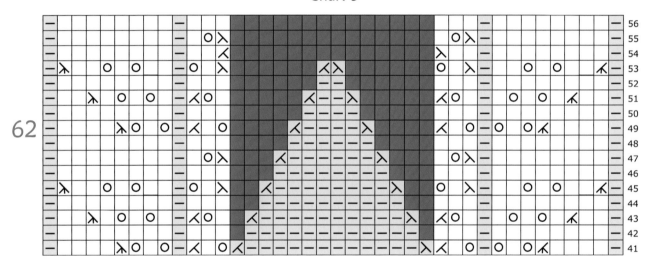

62

Chart 4

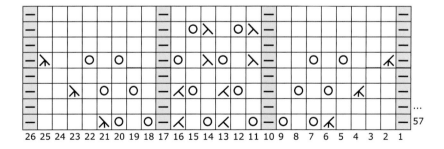

Round 2:

Instep stitches: follow chart3 beginning at round 41. (Note you are decreasing your heel flap gusset in the center portion of chart 3.) *Heel stitches*: K stockinette.

Remaining heel rounds:

Instep stitches: continue to follow chart3. *Heel stitches*: K stockinette.

repeat until you have 26 instep stitches and 43 heel stitches.

Foot:

Instep stitches: Follow chart 4 starting at lower right and moving to the left and up.
Heel stitches: K

Repeat until foot is the correct length to begin toe decreases (usually this is at base of big toe).

Toe:

Arrange stitches by slipping 4 stitches from the heel stitches to the beginning and end of instep stitches. You now have 34 instep stitches and 35 heel stitches.

Round 1:

K both instep and heel stitches

Round 2:

Instep stitches: K1, SSK, K to last 3 stitches, K2tog, K1.
Heel stitches: same as instep stitches.

Migration

This is a pretty little 2-color anklet worked in contrasting colors. The design on the top of the foot reminds me of the V-formation a flock of migrating birds makes. The rich prussian blue and lichen greens set off the intricate patterns well and impart a sense of movement throughout. These socks are knit from the toe up and feature a short row heel and patterned sole. The stranded colorwork makes these socks warm and cushiony. Knit them in your favorite color combination and let your feet's fancy take flight!

Migration Specs

Yarn requirements: approximately 200 yd ea of 2 colors of fingering weight sock yarn.

Yarn used: Chameleon Colorworks Footsie (70% superwash wool, 30% nylon), color: lichen (WPI = 16.5) and Trekking XXL (100% superwash wool), color 71 (WPI = 18.5), one skein each.

Needles: Size 1 circular or double pointed needles, or size to obtain correct gauge.

Gauge: 8.5 stitches, 12 rounds per inch (2.5 cm) in stranded colorwork knitting.

Notions: Stitch marker, tapestry needle.

Color Suggestions: Solid, Semi-solid or Painted. Colors should contrast well.

In the model shown, the yellow/green yarn is Color A and the blue yarn is Color B.

Cast On:

Holding two needles together, cast on 14 stitches in color A using a figure 8 cast on. Knit one side of the cast on with one needle and then the other side with a second needle. You now have 14 live stitches on either side of the cast on. One set of 14 is your instep stitches, and the other set is the heel sts (28 sts total).

Toe:

Round 1:

Knit instep and heel stitches

Round 2:

Instep stitches: K1, M1, K to one stitch before last stitch, M1, K1
Heel stitches: same as instep stitches.

Remaining toe rounds:

Repeat rounds 1 and 2 until you have 30 instep stitches and 30 heel stitches. Slip last heel stitch to instep stitches. You now have 31 instep and 29 heel stitches.

Foot:

Instep stitches: follow chart 1 starting at lower right and moving to the left and up.

heel stitches: follow chart 2.

When you have completed row 32 of chart 2, repeat row 32 until the foot measures to an inch less than your overall foot dimensions. You should begin the heel when you have about an inch of heel showing when trying the sock on.

Heel:

Short row heel is worked on heel stitches only.

Short row decreasing

Row 1: K 28 stitches. Bring yarn to front as if to purl and slip last stitch from left needle to right needle. Turn your work.

Row 2: Move yarn to front again as if to purl. Slip first stitch from left needle to right needle (the stitch that was unworked from the previous row). Purl next stitch. The yarn that you

Chart 1

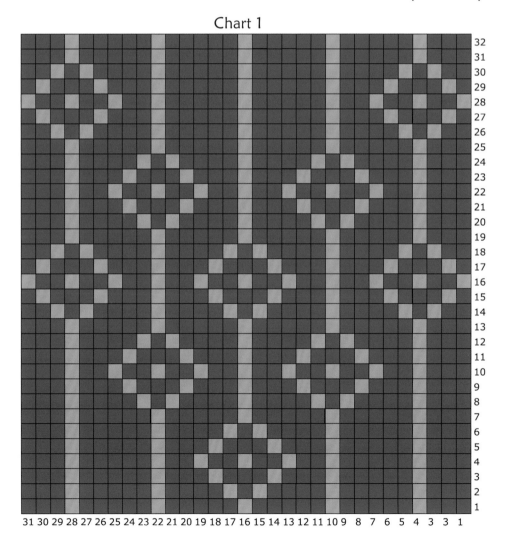

brought forward on the previous row and then forward on this row will have completely wrapped around the last stitch. This is called a wrap.

Purl across until one stitch remains unpurled. Bring yarn to back as if to knit and slip last stitch. Turn your work.

Row 3: Bring yarn to back as if to knit. Slip first stitch. You have wrapped that stitch. Knit across to the last stitch before the unworked stitch. Wrap and turn your work.

Row 4: Slip first stitch, purl across to stitch before the unworked stitch. Wrap and turn.

Repeat row 3 and 4 until you have 9 wrapped stitches on either end and 11 live stitches in the middle.

Short Row Increasing

Row 1: Knit all live stitches until you reach first wrapped stitch. Pick up the wrap and the stitch and knit them together. Wrap the next stitch (it will now have 2 wraps). Turn your work.

Row 2: Slip first stitch (the one with 2 wraps). Purl across to the first wrapped stitch. Pick up the wrap and the stitch and purl together. Wrap the next stitch (again it will have 2 wraps). Turn your work.

Row 3: Slip first stitch, knit across to next wrapped stitch. Pick up both wraps and the stitch and knit together. Wrap the next stitch and turn your work.

Row 4: Slip the first stitch, purl across to

next wrapped stitch. Pick up both wraps and the stitch and purl together. Wrap the next stitch and turn your work.

Repeat row 3 and 4 until you have picked up all of the wrapped stitches. You should now have 29 stitches on your heel needle.

Cuff

Instep and Heel stitches: Follow chart 3 starting at the lower left corner and working to the left and up. You will have 10 repeats of the pattern around the circumference of the sock. When you have completed row 8 of chart 3, begin again at row 1 and work 2 more repeats of the chart.

When 3 repeats of chart 3 are completed, work K2 P2 rib for 6 rounds.

Bind off using a sewn bind off.

Chart 2

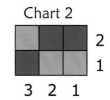

2
1

3 2 1

Chart 3

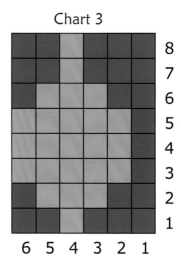

8
7
6
5
4
3
2
1

6 5 4 3 2 1

April Fools

An illusion knit that combines sideways construction, softly variegated hues and fun calf shaping, April Fools is a sock with sass! This sock is knit flat and grafted together into a tube then fitted with afterthought heel and toe. The shaping up the calf allows for perfect fit as well as optical interest. And the zing of complementary colors of red and green really allows this sock to sizzle. When viewed straight on, the eye sees vertical stripes, but turn it to a bit more oblique angle and you'll see horizontal stripes pop out. A perfect sock to wear on an April day when the green of spring has got you feeling a little foolish....

April Fools Specs

Yarn requirements: approximately 200 yd ea of 2 colors of fingering weight sock yarn.

Yarn used: Chameleon Colorworks Bambino (70% superwash merino, 30% bamboo), colors: Black Cherry, Moss, 1 skein each (WPI = 15.5)

Needles: Size 1 circular or straight needles, or size to obtain correct gauge. Same size dpns or circulars to knit toe, heel and ribbing.

Gauge: 7.5 stitches, 11 rounds per inch (2.5 cm) in stockinette.

Notions: Stitch marker, tapestry needle.

Color Suggestions: Solids or paints, contrasting colors.

Calculate Foot Length:

Using a hand knit sock that fits you well, measure distance from heel stitches to toe stitches on the bottom of the foot (see diagram on p. 13). Because you are knitting the sock sideways this is not readily adjustable area and it needs to be calculated ahead of time. When you have determined how many inches you need, multiply by 7.5 (stitches per inch) to determine how many stitches will make up the bottom of your foot. Round off to the nearest multiple of 5. If you are in the middle of 5, it is better to round up than to round down, you can adjust the overall length of the sock by decreasing the toe either faster or slower to shorten or lengthen the toe.

In the model for this pattern color A is Black Cherry, color B is Moss

Cast On:

With waste yarn, provisionally cast on your number of foot stitches plus 45 stitches. Round up or down to nearest multiple of 5 [for size 7 ladies I used 80] and add or subtract those stitches to make the overall number of stitches a multiple of 5. K 3 rows stockinette.

Knit Front of Sock:

Change to color A and knit illusion stripe pattern for 38 rows ending with Color A. Break Color B.

70

> Illusion Stripe Pattern:
>
> This is a four row pattern with an alternating set of purls in each color.
>
> Starting on right side
> Row 1: (Color A) K
> Row 2: (Color A) *P 5, K 5 repeat from * to end of row
> Row 3: (Color B) K
> Row 4: (Color B) *K5 P 5 repeat from * to end of row

Divide for Foot and Cuff:

Knit bottom of foot:

With right side facing you K one row with color B. Purl back only the number of stitches you calculated for your foot length (point F in the diagram) [for size 7 ladies I used 35 stitches]. Continue on in stockinette stitch for another 36 rows (38 rows total) making the foot flap in color B. Do not knit the rest of the stitches on the needle (if you wish you can remove those stitches to a holding piece of waste yarn).

Break color B. Move foot stitches to a piece of waste yarn to hold in place while you knit cuff.

Knit back of cuff:

Beginning with color B on wrong side of knitting at point F in the diagram, work row 4 of the illusion stripe pattern in color B on the remaining stitches (the non-foot stitches). Continue in illusion stripe pattern as established for another 15 rows, ending with row 3 of the illusion stripe pattern (color B). Place the last 10 stitches on spare circular needle. Break color B.

Begin short row shaping:

Short row increasing
Row 2
From wrong side, work row 4 of illusion stripe pattern starting in color B (35 stitches).

Row 3
Work row 1 of illusion stripe pattern for 34 stitches, turn work.

Row 4
Slip first 2 stitches (1 stitch color B, 1 stitch color A) then continue row 2 of illusion stripe pattern (2 slips + 33 stitches).

Row 5
Work row 3 of illusion stripe pattern for 32 stitches, break color B.

Place last 10 stitches on spare needle (3 slipped stitches + 8 stitches in color B).

Row 6
From wrong side, work row 4 of illusion stripe pattern starting in color B (25 stitches).

Row 7
Work row 1 of illusion stripe pattern for 24 stitches, turn work.

Row 8
Slip first 2 stitches (1 stitch color B, 1 stitch color A) then continue row 2 of illusion stripe pattern (2 slips + 23 stitches).

Row 9
Work row 3 of illusion stripe pattern for 22 stitches, break color B.

Place last 10 stitches on spare needle (3 slipped stitches + 8 stitches in color B).

Row 10
From wrong side, work row 4 of illusion stripe pattern starting in color B (15 stitches).

Row 11
Work row 1 of illusion stripe pattern for 14 stitches, turn work.

Row 12
Slip first 2 stitches (1 stitch color B, 1 stitch color A) then continue row 2 of illusion stripe pattern (2 slips + 23 stitches).

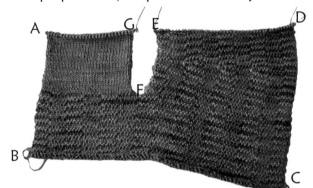

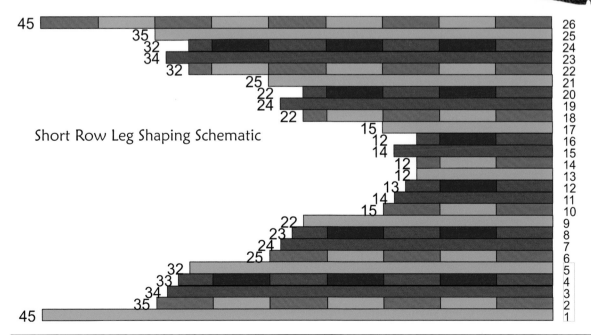

Short Row Leg Shaping Schematic

Row 13-14
Work row 3 and 4 of illusion stripe pattern for 12 stitches.

Short row decreasing

Row 15
Work row 1 of illusion stripe pattern for 14 stitches, turn work.

Row 16
Slip first 2 stitches then continue row 2 of illusion stripe pattern (2 slips + 12 stitches).

Row 17
Work row 3 of illusion stripe pattern for 15 stitches, break color B.

Row 18
From wrong side slip 10 stitches from spare needle back to working needle. Work row 4 of illusion stripe pattern for 22 stitches

Row 19
Work row 1 of illusion stripe pattern for 24 stitches, turn work.

Row 20
Slip first 2 stitches then continue row 2 of illusion stripe pattern (2 slips + 22 stitches).

Row 21
Work row 3 of illusion stripe pattern for 25 stitches, break color B.

Row 22
From wrong side slip 10 stitches from spare needle back to working needle. Work row 4 of illusion stripe pattern for 32 stitches.

Row 23
Work row 1 of illusion stripe pattern for 34 stitches, turn work.

Row 24
Slip first 2 stitches then continue row 2 of illusion stripe pattern (2 slips + 32 stitches).

Row 25
Work row 3 of illusion stripe pattern for 35 stitches, break color B.

Row 26
From wrong side slip last 10 stitches from spare needle back to working needle. Work row 4 of illusion stripe pattern for 45 stitches. This completes the short row leg shaping.

Remainder of back of cuff

Continue knitting across all stitches in shadow stripe pattern for 15 more rows ending with color B. You have only done one row of color B at this point. The second row will be the grafting row.

Graft sock into a tube:

Lay sock on table with right side face down. Fold foot section and cuff section over so that instep stitches are facing the table and bottom of foot and back of cuff are face up. Your color B yarn is on the left of the knitting and your provisional cast on is at the bottom face down. Measure off approx 30" of color B yarn and break yarn. Remove provisional cast on yarn and place live stitches on a circular needle or piece of yarn.

Grafting cuff. The direction of your grafting changes on the top stitches (back of cuff) but is always the same on the bottom stitches (front of cuff). For grafting instructions see diagrams in the techniques section on page 92.

Graft 5 st in garter stitch (purlwise on top and knitwise on bottom).

Graft next 5 stitches in knit stitch (knitwise on top and knitwise on bottom).

Continue in this manner alternating every 5 stitches until cuff is grafted.

Grafting foot. Graft entire foot in knit stitch (knitwise on top and knitwise on bottom). Pull yarn through last loop twice.

Toe:

At toe end of sock, pick up 48 stitches evenly spaced, 24 instep stitches and 24 heel stitches.

Round 1:

K both instep and heel stitches

Round 2:

Instep stitches: K1, SSK, K to last 3 stitches, K2tog, K1.
Heel stitches: same as instep stitches.

Repeat rounds 1 and 2 until you have 12 instep and heel stitches. Graft toe closed.

Heel:

At toe end of sock, pick up 48 stitches evenly spaced, 24 top stitches and 24 bottom stitches.

Round 1:

K both instep and heel stitches

Round 2:

Top stitches: K1, SSK, K to last 3 stitches, K2tog, K1.
Bottom stitches: same as top stitches.

Repeat rounds 1 and 2 until you have 12 instep and heel stitches. Graft heel closed.

Cuff ribbing:

At the top of the cuff Pick up 68 stitches spaced evenly.

K2 P2 rib for 6 rounds. Bind off using picot bind off.

Picot bind off:

*Cast on 2 stitches onto left needle using the slip stitch cast on.

bind off 4 stitches using the usual method.

Slip the single stitch on the right hand needle back onto the left hand needle.*

Repeat from * to * until end of round.

Kristallen

In Norwegian "kristallen" means crystals. These socks are named for the beautiful 4-fold symmetry of the main motif which looks a bit like a snow-flake. Whatever you like to call them, crystals or snowflakes, this sock was inspired by traditional Norwegian motifs and colors. The beautiful Trekking Pro Natura yarn has a shimmer of bamboo that gives it just the right frosty look for a crystalline winter morning.

Kristallen Specs

Yarn requirements: approximately 450 yd of fingering weight sock yarn.

Yarn used: Trekking XXL Pro Natura (75% superwash wool, 25% line bamboo fiber), color 1509 (color A), 1501 (color B), 1601 (color C) (WPI = 18.5), one skein each

Needles: Size 1 circular or double pointed needles, or size to obtain correct gauge.

Gauge: 8.5 stitches, 10 rounds per inch (2.5 cm) in 2 color stranded knitting.

Notions: Stitch marker, tapestry needle.

Color Suggestions: solid or semi solid, and hand painted.

Cast On

Using a long tail cast on, the slip knot cast on, or your favorite flexible cast on, cast on 68 stitches in color A, and join in a round, taking care not to twist your work.

Cuff

Divide stitches in half and distribute in two sets of stitches, instep sts (34 sts), and heel sts (34 sts).

Work K2 P2 rib for 9 rounds.

Rounds 1-53:

K 1 round in stockinette, increasing by 4 stitches to 72 stitches total.

Join Color B. Follow chart 1 starting at lower right and moving to the left and up. Repeat the chart 2 times around the circumference of the sock. When you finish round 53, begin heel.

Heel:

Heel flap:

Work heel flap back and forth on heel stitches only. Move 1 stitch at the beginning of the instep stitches to the heel stitches. You now have 31 heel stitches and 29 instep stitches. Work heel in stripe pattern as follows *K1 color A, K2 color C. Repeat from * 10 times, K1 color A. Continue in stripe pattern for 17 rows.

Chart 1

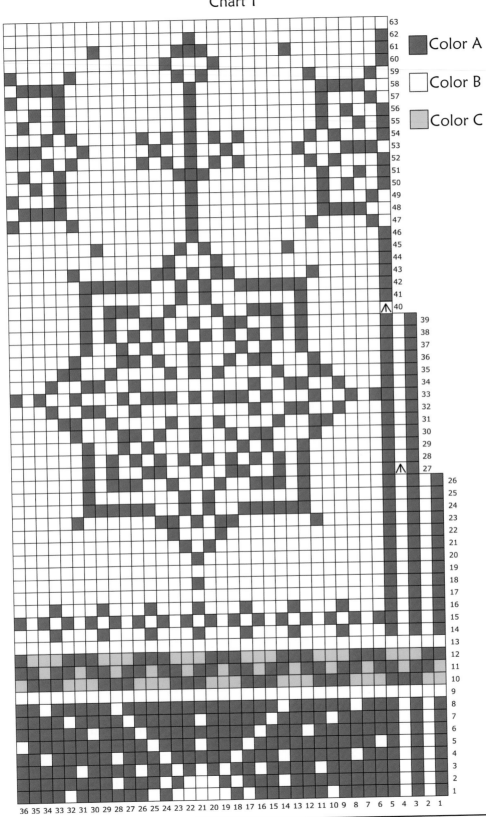

Color A
Color B
Color C

Turn Heel:

Work heel turn in color C.

Row 1: Sl 1, knit until 8 stitches remain on left hand needle, ssk, k1, turn.

Row 2: Sl 1, purl until 8 stitches remain on left hand needle, p2tog, p1, turn.

Row 3: Sl 1, knit until 6 stitches remain on left hand needle (1 st before the gap made by turning), ssk, k1, turn.

Row 4: Sl 1, purl until 6 stitches remain on left hand needle (1 st before the gap made by turning), p2tog, p1, turn.

Row 5: Sl 1, knit until 4 stitches remain on left hand needle (1 st before the gap made by turning), ssk, k1, turn.

Row 6: Sl 1, purl until 4 stitches remain on left hand needle (1 st before the gap made by turning), p2tog, p1, turn.

Row 7: Sl 1, knit until 2 stitches remain on left hand needle (1 st before the gap made by turning), ssk, turn.

Row 8: Sl 1, purl until 2 stitches remain on left hand needle (1 st before the gap made by turning), p2tog, turn,

You should have 23 heel stitches. Knit across all 23 heel stitches.

Gusset:

Round 1: With heel needle and color A pick up 15 sts (or appropriate number for your adjusted heel flap depth) on left side of the heel flap you just made.

Work across instep stitches in stockinette using color A.

With a spare needle pick up 15 (or same number you picked up on the left side) stitches on right side of heel flap and transfer to heel needle. Knit to end of heel stitches.

Round 2:
Instep stitches: continue in stockinette.
Heel stitches: K1, SSK, K to last 3 sts of needle; k2 tog, K 1.

Round 3:
Instep stitches: continue in stockinette
Heel stitches: K

Repeat rounds 2 and 3 until you have 31 heel stitches.

Foot:

Instep and heel stitches: K stockinette in color A until foot is the correct length to begin toe shaping (usually this is at base of big toe).

Toe:

Move 1 stitch at end of heel stitches back to beginning of instep stitches. K instep and heel stitches in same stripe pattern as heel flap beginning with color A and ending with 2nd stitch of color C,

Round 1:
Instep and heel stitches: K in stripe pattern.

Round 2:
Instep stitches: (in stripe pattern) K1, SSK, K to last 2 stitches, K2tog.
Heel stitches: same as instep stitches.

First stitch of heel or instep stitches is always color A, second stitch and last stitch (including decreases) is always color C. Repeat rounds 1 and 2 until you have 14 stitches per needle. Graft toe closed using color A.

Koi

When I was a child, my neighbor across the street had a koi pond. Every afternoon in the summer we would traipse across to eat oranges off of her tree and feed her fish. I loved watching the beautiful rainbow colored fish swimming right near the surface, opening their little mouths for our fishy treats. This pattern was inspired by the beautiful colors in the trekking sock yarn which reminded me of the brightly colored koi in the blue water. I created a stitch pattern that reminded me of fish scales, and ended up with this wonderfully textured rainbow sock! Create your own koi in shades of your choosing. It's easy to extend or crop the pattern to make the sock longer or shorter.

Koi Specs

Yarn requirements: approximately 350 yd of fingering weight sock yarn.

Yarn used: Zitron Trekking XXL (100% superwash wool), color 108, 1 skein (WPI = 18.5)

Needles: Size 1 circular or double pointed needles, or size to obtain correct gauge.

Gauge: 7.5 stitches, 10.5 rounds per inch (2.5 cm) in stockinette.

Notions: Stitch marker, tapestry needle.

Color Suggestions: Hand painted, or rainbow.

Cast On

Using a long tail cast on, the slip knot cast on, or your favorite flexible cast on, cast on 60 stitches and join in a round, taking care not to twist your work.

Cuff

Divide stitches in half and distribute in two sets of stitches, instep sts (36 sts), and heel sts (24 sts).

Rounds 1-16: Round 1 P2 K2 15 tims around. Thereafter follow chart 1 starting at lower right corner and working to the left and up.

Rounds 17-57: follow chart 2 starting at the bottom right and moving to the left and up. Repeat the chart 5 times around the sock's circumference. When chart 2 is completed, begin again at row 1 and work for 25 more repeats.

Heel:

Short row heel is worked on heel stitches only.

Short row decreasing

Row 1: K 23 stitches. Bring yarn to front as if to purl and slip last stitch from left needle to right needle. Turn your work.

Row 2: Move yarn to front again as if to purl. Slip first stitch from left needle to right needle (the stitch that was unworked from the previous row). Purl next stitch. The yarn that you brought forward on the previous row and then forward on this row will have completely wrapped around the last stitch. This is called a wrap.

Purl across until one stitch remains unpurled. Bring yarn to back as if to knit and slip last stitch. Turn your work.

Row 3: Bring yarn to back as if to knit. Slip first stitch. You have wrapped that stitch. Knit across to the last stitch before the unworked stitch. Wrap and turn your work.

Row 4: Slip first stitch, purl across to stitch before the unworked stitch. Wrap and turn.

Repeat row 3 and 4 until you have 8 wrapped stitches on either end and 8 live stitches in the middle.

Short Row Increasing

Row 1: Knit all live stitches until you reach first wrapped stitch. Pick up the wrap and the stitch and knit them together. Wrap the next stitch (it will now have 2 wraps). Turn your work.

Row 2: Slip first stitch (the one with 2 wraps). Purl across to the first wrapped stitch. Pick up the wrap and the stitch and purl together. Wrap the next stitch (again it will have 2 wraps). Turn your work.

Row 3: Slip first stitch, knit across to next wrapped stitch. Pick up both wraps and the stitch and knit together. Wrap the next stitch and turn your work.

Row 4: Slip the first stitch, purl across to next wrapped stitch. Pick up both wraps and the stitch and purl together. Wrap the next stitch and turn your work.

Repeat row 3 and 4 until you have picked up all of the wrapped stitches. You should now have 24 stitches on your heel needle.

80

Foot:

Continue to follow chart 2 on instep needle(s), K stockinette on heel needle(s), until foot is the correct length to begin toe decreases (usually this is at base of big toe).

Toe:

Round 1:

K both instep and heel stitches

Round 2:

Instep stitches: K1, SSK, K to last 3 stitches, K2tog, K1.
Heel stitches: same as instep stitches.

Repeat rounds 1 and 2 until you have 14 stitches per needle.
Graft toe closed.

Chart 1

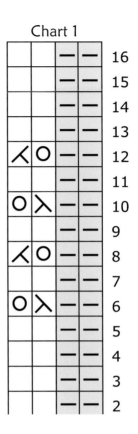

Chart 2

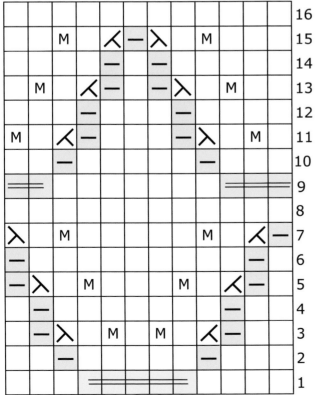

A note about stitch clusters....

Chart 1 has 2 symbols for 5 stitch clusters. Although the blue cluster symbols occur at the edges of the chart, they are to be combined with the cluster symbol of the next chart repeat to make a 5 stitch cluster. When the 5 stitch cluster occurs at the beginning of the round, slip the last 2 stitches of the previous round onto the left needle and make the cluster at the beginning of the round. At the end of the round, slip the 2 stitches back.

Josephine

Oh la la! A two color sock with a regal flare, Josephine is named after the wife of Napoleon, the empress Josephine. These socks are extra warm because knitting in two colors means twice the layers of wool. They would be equally great inside of boots on a snowy winter morning, or peeking out through your birkenstocks on a spring day. These socks feature a mirrored crown-like image and a patterned sole. Wear your Josephine socks when you need a little extra luxury.

Josephine Specs

Yarn requirements: approximately 200 yd ea of 2 colors of fingering weight sock yarn.

Yarn used: Zitron Trekking XXL (100% superwash wool), color: 298 (WPI = 18.5), one skein Brown Sheep Wildfoote (100% superwash wool), color Ragtime (WPI = 16), one skein

Needles: Size 1 circular or double pointed needles, or size to obtain correct gauge.

Gauge: 30 stitches and 40 rounds = 10 cm (4 inches)

Notions: Stitch marker, tapestry needle

Color Suggestions: Solids or Semi-solids

In the model shown, color A is the grey, color B is red.

Cast On

Holding two needles together, using color 1, cast on 13 stitches using a figure 8 cast on. Knit one side of the cast on with one needle and then the other side with a second needle. You now have 13 live stitches on either side of the cast on. One set of 13 is your instep stitches, and the other set is the heel sts (26 sts total)

Toe:

Round 1: K

Round 2: On instep stitches K1, M1, K to one stitch before last stitch, M1, K1. Repeat on heel stitches

Chart 1

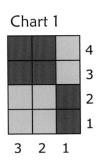

3   2   1

Rounds 3-16: repeat rounds 1 and 2 until you have 29 stitches on the heel stitch set and 29 stitches on the instep stitch set.

Join color B and knit 1 round

Foot:

Instep stitches: Follow chart two starting at bottom right and working to the left and up. (When you reach row 41 follow chart one in reverse from row 40 back through row 2. Do not duplicate row 41.

Heel stitches: Follow chart one starting at bottom right and working to the left and up.

Continue until you are about 1" from heel.

Heel:

Short row heel is worked on heel stitches only.

Short row decreasing

Row 1: K 28 stitches. Bring yarn to front as if to purl and slip last stitch from left needle to right needle. Turn your work.

Row 2: Move yarn to front again as if to purl. Slip first stitch from left needle to right needle (the stitch that was unworked from the previous row). Purl next stitch. The yarn that you brought forward on the previous row and then forward on this row will have completely wrapped around the last stitch. This is called a wrap.

Purl across until one stitch remains unpurled. Bring yarn to back as if to knit and slip last stitch. Turn your work.

Row 3: Bring yarn to back as if to knit. Slip first stitch. You have wrapped that stitch. Knit across to the last stitch before the unworked stitch. Wrap and turn.

Row 4: Slip first stitch, purl across to stitch before the unworked stitch. Wrap and turn.

Repeat row 3 and 4 until you have 8 wrapped stitches on either end and 8 live stitches in the middle.

Short Row Increasing

Row 1: Knit all live stitches until you reach first wrapped stitch. Pick up the wrap and the stitch and knit them together. Wrap the next stitch (it will now have 2 wraps). Turn your work.

Row 2: Slip first stitch (the one with 2 wraps). Purl across to the first wrapped stitch. Pick up the wrap and the stitch and purl together. Wrap the next stitch (again it will have 2 wraps). Turn your work.

Row 3: Slip first stitch, knit across to next wrapped stitch. Pick up both wraps and the stitch and knit together. Wrap the next stitch and turn your work.

Row 4: Slip the first stitch, purl across to next wrapped stitch. Pick up both wraps and the stitch and purl together. Wrap the next stitch and turn your work.

Repeat row 3 and 4 until you have picked up all of the wrapped stitches. You should now have 29 stitches on your heel needle.

Cuff

Continue following Chart one on instep stitches. Pick up at the row on chart one and repeat chart on heel stitches. When chart is completed, begin K1 P1 ribbing until cuff reaches desired length.

Bind off using a sewn bind off.

Chart 2

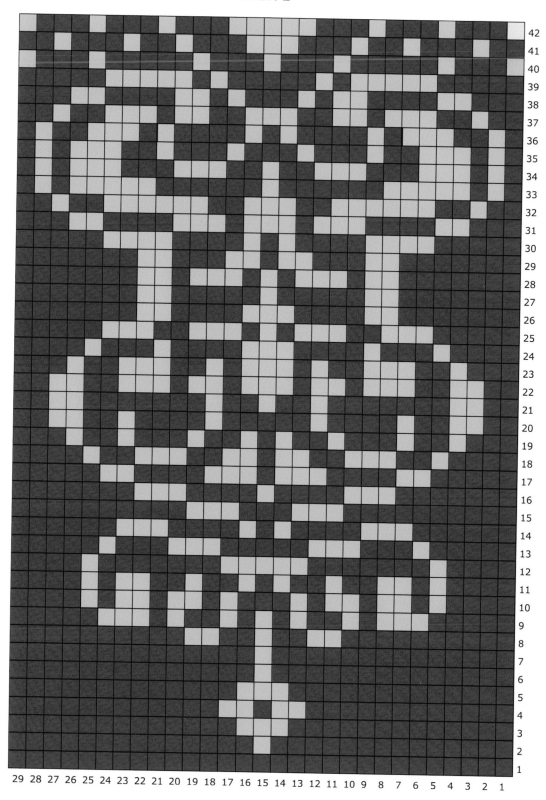

Chart Key & Techniques

☐	Knit	right cross 1 stitch purl cable
☐ (—)	Purl	left cross 1 stitch knit cable
■	No Stitch	left 2 over 1 cable cross purl
☐ (ℓ)	Knit through back loop	right 2 over 1 cable cross purl
☐ (⅄)	left leaning decrease	right cross 2 stitch knit cable
☐ (⅄)	right leaning decrease	left 1 over 2 cable
☐ (⅄)	left leaning double decrease	right 1 over 2 cable
☐ (⅄)	right leaning double decrease	4 stitch cluster over Ktbl, p2, ktbl
☐ (Λ)	centered double decrease	7 stitch cluster over Ktbl, p2, Ktbl, p2, Ktbl
☐ (/•)	purl decrease	4 stitch cluster over K4
☐ (O)	yarn over	5 stitch cluster over K5
☐ (M)	make one	5 stitch cluster over K5
☐ (V̇)	make one purl	3 stitch cluster over P3
☐ (V)	make one knit in front and back	2 stitch cluster over P2
	left cross 1 stitch purl cable	

Long Tail Cast On

The long tail cast on is a very useful method of casting on. It's drawbacks are that it requires a long tail and cannot be easily used in the middle of your knitting.

Take needle over yarn coming from top of index finger and through the thumb loop.

Reach your needle under the yarn and pull it through the loop

drape yarn over index finger and thumb catching tails with your pinkie

Pull on the long tail to cinch up the stitch.

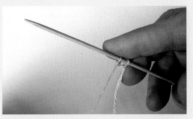

Hold your index finger on top of the yarn you just pulled through the loop. Make sure the yarn is close to the stitch next to it.

Insert knitting needle under the yarn spanning between the thumb and index finger and hold in place with your right hand index finger.

Slip Knot Cast On

The slip knot cast on has the advantage that it doesn't require a pre-measured tail. It's important to pay attention to the tension in the last step to make this method work.

Your finished cast on stitch is basically a second slip knot.

Insert the needle under the loop around the thumb

Begin with a regular slip knot followed by an inverted loop over the needle.

Figure 8 Cast On

The figure 8 cast on is a really nice method to begin a toe-up sock. It leaves a seamless closure of the tube when knitting in the round. This method works easiest with circular needles because of the flexibility of the cable but it can be accomplished on double points as well.

Snug the figure 8 loops up next to each other and tighten if necessary.

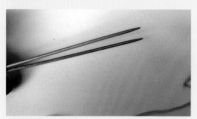

Begin by holding two needles side by side.

Lay the yarn over both of the needles, and bring it under the top needle.

Bring the yarn up between the needles and over the bottom needle. Then bring the yarn around the bottom needle and back up through the needles, then over and around the top needle again, weaving a figure 8 around the two needles.

Enter the loops on the top needle knitwise and knit them off. Next, flip the two needles around, keeping the right side facing up to you. Enter the loops on the other needle from the right hand side and knit them through the back loop.

If you are using double points, transfer half of the stitches on each needle to another needle (4 needles total) to make knitting in the round easier.

 ## No Stitch

When this symbol occurs in a chart it means no stitch occurring there. It is only a placeholder to keep the chart easy to read.

 ## Knit

On the front side of your knitting, enter the front of the stitch from the left side, then pull yarn through loop.

— Purl

On the back side of your knitting, enter the back of the stitch from the right side, then wrap yarn around needle and pull yarn through loop.

ℓ Knit Through Back Loop

Knitting through the back loop results in a tight, well defined stitch.

Enter stitch from right side instead of left side to knit. This produces a twisted stitch.

⊠ Left Leaning Decrease

The left leaning decrease is also commonly called SSK which stands for slip, slip, knit.

Enter the first stitch on the left hand needle from the left (knitwise) and slip it to the right needle. Likewise slip the second stitch. Place both stitches back on the left hand needle and knit them together, entering both stitches at the same time from the right side and knitting through the back loop.

⊠ Right Leaning Decrease

The right leaning decrease is commonly called K2tog which stands for knit two together.

Enter both stitches on the left hand needle from the left (knitwise) and knit them together.

⊠ Left Leaning Double Decrease

The left leaning double decrease is worked similarly to the SSK, only slipping 3 stitches instead of 2

Enter the first stitch on the left hand needle from the left (knitwise) and slip it to the right needle. Likewise slip the second and third stitch. Place all three stitches back on the left hand needle and knit them together, entering all three stitches at the same time from the right side.

⊠ Right Leaning Double Decrease

The right leaning double decrease is worked similarly to the K2tog, only working 3 stitches instead of 2

⊠ Purl Decrease

The purl decrease is worked similarly to the K2tog, only from the purl side.

Enter 2 stitches at the same time and purl them together.

⊠ Centered Double Decrease

A centered double decrease is an elegant way to knit 3 together with the middle stitch on top leaving a nice centered "spine" on the stitch.

Enter the first 2 stitches knitwise as if to do a K2tog, but instead just slip them to the right hand needle.

Knit the next stitch off the left hand needle.

Pass both of the slipped stitches together over the just knit stitch.

Yarn Over

The yarn over is a way to make a hole in your knitting for lace and eyelet patterns.

Bring yarn to front of knitting then over right needle.

K the next stitch on the left hand needle.

The yarn over makes an extra stitch in your knitting with a resultant hole below.

M Make 1

The make 1 is a method to increase your stitches without leaving a hole.

With the right hand needle pick up the ladder bar in between the stitches from the row below, entering from the back side.

Knit through the back loop to form a twisted stitch anchored in between your stitches.

V Make 1 knit in front & back

Similar to Make 1 (purl) knit into the forward and back loop of the same stitch to make one.

V̇ Make 1 (purl)

Make 1 in a purl section is a good way to increase your stitches less visibly.

With the right hand needle purl through the front leg of the stitch. Do not remove the stitch from your left hand needle.

Using the right hand needle, again purl through the stitch, this time through the back leg of the stitch.

You now have 2 purl stitches from one stitch.

One Stitch Cables

The one stitch cables are often called twisted stitches, but that can be confused with knitting through the back loop which is also called a twisted stitch. We define it as a one stitch cable, which is more accurate.

 Left Cross 1 stitch Purl Cable

The left cross one stitch purl cable is a way to move a single stitch from the right to the left on a purl background.

Place one stitch on a cable needle and hold in front of your work. Purl the next stitch.

Slip the stitch on the cable needle back to the left hand needle.

Knit the crossed stitch off.

Right Cross 1 stitch Purl

The right cross one stitch purl cable is a way to move a single stitch from the left to the right on a purl background.

Place one stitch on a cable needle and hold in back of your work. Knit the next stitch.

Slip the stitch on the cable needle back to the left hand needle.

Purl the crossed stitch off.

Left Cross 1 stitch Knit Cable

The left cross one stitch knit cable is a way to cross two knit stitches. The cross will appear to cross to the left because the right hand stitch is on top.

Work similarly to the Left Cross 1 Stitch Purl Cable.

Place one stitch on a cable needle and hold in front of your work.

Knit the next stitch.

Slip the stitch on the cable needle back to the left hand needle.

Knit the crossed stitch off.

Left 1 over 2 Cable

Work similarly to the Left Cross 1 Stitch Purl Cable.

Place one stitch on a cable needle and hold in front of your work.

Knit the next 2 stitches.

Slip the stitch on the cable needle back to the left hand needle.

Knit the crossed stitch off.

Right 1 over 2 Cable

Work similarly to the Right Cross 1 Stitch Purl Cable.

Place two stitches on a cable needle and hold in back of your work.

Knit the next stitch.

Slip the stitches on the cable needle back to the left hand needle.

Knit the crossed stitches off.

Left 2 over 1 Cable Cross

The left 2 over 1 cable cross is a way to move two stitches from the right to the left on a purl background.

Place two stitches on a cable needle and hold in front of your work. Purl the next stitch.

Slip the stitches on the cable needle back to the left hand needle.

Knit the crossed stitches off.

Right 2 over 1 Cable Cross

The right 2 over 1 cable cross is a way to move two stitches from the left to the right on a purl background.

Place one stitch on a cable needle and hold in back of your work. Knit the next two stitches.

Slip the stitch on the cable needle back to the left hand needle.

Purl the crossed stitch off.

Right 2 over 2 Cable Cross

The right 2 over 2 cable cross is a way to make a two stitch wide cable cross which appears to cross to the right.

Place two stitches on a cable needle and hold in back of your work. Knit the next 2 stitches.

Slip the stitches on the cable needle back to the left hand needle.

Knit the crossed stitches off.

Grafting (Kitchener Stitch)

Grafting, or Kitchener Stitch, is a way of sewing two live rows of stitches closed so that the appearance of the sewing is seamless. For most applications like sewing up toes, or other seams you will use the knit stitch graft method. For the April Fools sock you will also need the garter stitch graft method.

For either method arrange both sides of knitting so that the right side is facing up and the live stitches are facing each other.

Knit Stitch Grafting

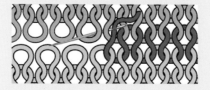

Using a tapestry needle threaded with the working yarn, come up through the back of stitch number one of the lower row of stitches.

Insert the needle from the front through stitch number one of the upper row of stitches.

Bring the needle back up through stitch two of the upper row from the back side.

Insert the needle from the front through stitch number one of the lower row of stitches.

Bring the needle back up through stitch two of the lower row from the back side.

Continue in this fashion until all live stitches have been sewn together. If necessary, snug the stitches by gently pulling on the sewing yarn.

Garter Stitch Grafting

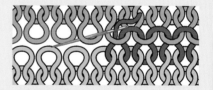

Using a tapestry needle threaded with the working yarn, come up through the back of stitch number one of the lower row of stitches.

Insert the needle from the back through stitch number one of the upper row of stitches.

Bring the needle down through stitch two of the upper row from the front.

Insert the needle from the front through stitch number one of the lower row of stitches.

Bring the needle back up through stitch two of the lower row from the back side.

Continue in this fashion until all live stitches have been sewn together. If necessary, snug the stitches by gently pulling on the sewing yarn.

Clustered Stitches

Stitch clusters are indicated on the charts by 2 bars across the stitches and a yellow background. In each case you are meant to cluster the stitches and then work them according to the underlying stitch designation on the chart.

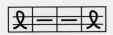

Cluster 4 stitches, then Ktbl, P 2, Ktbl

Cluster 2 stitches, then P 2

Cluster 3 stitches, then P 3

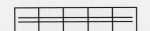

Cluster 5 stitches, then K 5

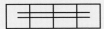

Cluster 4 stitches, then K 4

When clustered stitches occur at the edge of the chart they are colored blue to indicate that they should be combined with the blue cluster at the beginning of the next chart repeat to give a larger cluster.

The 3 stitch cluster and the 2 stitch cluster should be combined to give a 5 stitch cluster. Cluster all 5 stitches, then K 5.

When the 5 stitch cluster occurs at the beginning of the round, slip the last 2 stitches of the previous round onto the left needle and make the cluster at the beginning of the round. At the end of the round, slip the 2 stitches back.

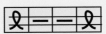

The 4 stitch cluster and the 3 stitch cluster should be combined to give a 7 stitch cluster. Cluster all 7 stitches, then Ktbl, P2, Ktbl, P2, Ktbl.

When the 7 stitch cluster occurs at the beginning of the round, slip the last 3 stitches of the previous round onto the left needle and make the cluster at the beginning of the round. At the end of the round, slip the 3 stitches back.

Making a Cluster

Move the appropriate number of stitches you are clustering to a cable needle

Starting from the back bring the yarn around the cable needle twice. Do not pull tight.

Slip the clustered stitches back onto the left hand needle.

Work the clustered stitches according to the underlying stitch designation on the chart.

Resources

Yarn companies

Brown Sheep Company
www.brownsheep.com

Chameleon Colorworks
www.chameleoncolorworks.com

Jojoland
www.jojoland.com

Yarn Love
www.shopyarnlove.com

Zitron Trekking
www.skacelknitting.com

94

Internet Resources

Knitting instruction
http://www.knittingatknoon.com

Knitting yarn, pattern and other reviews
http://www.knittersreview.com

My every intention is that there be no errors in this manuscript. Nevertheless, errors can occur. For updates or errata, please check the website at www.rustlingleafpress.com

Text, Illustration and photos (except where noted) by Janel Laidman.
Book layout and design by Janel Laidman
Cover design by Janel Laidman
Printed by Friesens Printing, Manitoba, Canada

Text typefont: Maiandra GD Open type version
Caption typefont: Verdana Open type version

Photo credits: stock photos from www.iStockphoto.com

p 15 Ingmar Wesemann
p 16 Grafissimo
p 20 angelmanuelherrero
p 20 nojustice
p 25 Ken Pilon
p 26 and 31 Greg Marshall
p 26 William Bullimore
p 32 Yuriy Soshnikov
p 36 Sharon Day
p 46 Brasil2
p 52 Kirill Volkov
p 64 Kevin Miller
p 78 norcon
p 82 naphtalina